AF481311

Knife Making
for Kids

Step by step to getting started
in knifemaking for kids

Copyright © 2020

All rights reserved. No part of this guide may be reproduced in any form without permission in writing from the publisher except in the case of brief quotations embodied in critical articles or reviews.

Legal & Disclaimer

The information contained in this book and its contents is not designed to replace or take the place of any form of medical or professional advice; and is not meant to replace the need for independent medical, financial, legal or other professional advice or services, as may be required. The content and information in this book has been provided for educational and entertainment purposes only.

The content and information contained in this book has been compiled from sources deemed reliable, and it is accurate to the best of the Author's knowledge, information and belief. However, the Author cannot guarantee its accuracy and validity and cannot be held liable for any errors and/or omissions. Further, changes are periodically made to this book as and when needed. Where appropriate and/or necessary, you must consult a professional (including but not limited to your doctor, attorney, financial advisor or such other professional advisor) before using any of the suggested remedies, techniques, or information in this book.

Upon using the contents and information contained in this book, you agree to hold harmless the Author from and against any damages, costs, and expenses, including any legal fees potentially resulting from the application of any of the information provided by this book. This disclaimer applies to any loss, damages or injury caused by the use and application, whether directly or indirectly, of any advice or information presented, whether for breach of contract, tort, negligence, personal injury, criminal intent, or under any other cause of action.

You agree to accept all risks of using the information presented inside this book.

You agree that by continuing to read this book, where appropriate and/or necessary, you shall consult a professional (including but not limited to your doctor, attorney, or financial advisor or such other advisor as needed) before using any of the suggested remedies, techniques, or information in this book.

TABLE OF CONTENTS

INTRODUCTION

Today's blacksmiths provide essentially the same functions that their trade has performed for countless generations. Modern blacksmiths routinely create things like coat racks, hinges, tools, weapons, furniture, even custom projects and art pieces. A quality handmade product is just as in demand today as it was 200 years ago, it is just harder to come by.

What's more, one branch of blacksmithing known as farriery (making and fitting custom horseshoes) requires a mastery of the craft and can never be replaced. Mass produced horseshoes still need to be modified and fitted to each specific horse, something that a farrier, can ensure means a horse remains healthy and does not end up lame as a result of poor shoes.

The modern blacksmith's shop also hasn't changed much in the last few hundred years. While there are a wide variety of forge-types available (see chapter 3) the old ways are still often the best ways which means workshops are dark, loud and dirty because the best work comes from using charcoal for fuel. Workshops are dark so that the blacksmith can tell the current temperature of the metal they are working with and charcoal provides the best, most manageable heat. Both are required to ensure each item made is heated to the ideal temperature to ensure it remains as strong as possible for as long as possible.

Coal began to replace charcoal as the most common type of fuel used for blacksmithing as deforestation became more of an issue worldwide. Coal is less ideal for blacksmithing as a large portion of the coal on Earth contains too much sulfur to be useful for blacksmithing. Too much sulfur in the coal causes both steel and iron to crumble rather than become malleable when exposed to heat. If you plan on using coal as a fuel source, always make sure to check the sulfur levels first.

A long history

Up until the industrial revolution, every village and town had at least one blacksmith. Mass production meant that many of the tools which up until that point were made by hand exclusively by blacksmiths were now made in factories. Prior to this, blacksmiths worldwide spent their time hammering and heating iron, unaware of the chemical changes they were causing to take place in the iron. What they did know is how this improved the strength of the items they created.

This holds true today as this process pulls any excess oxygen out of the metal, preventing it from rusting while at the same time adding additional carbon which made the iron stronger. This is how steel is made and is an important part of the blacksmith's art.

As late as the 1850's armies worldwide still employed blacksmiths to repair things like artillery, horse tack, wagons and horseshoes. These blacksmiths worked out of forges built into the backs of wagons and it was not uncommon for each regiment to have at least one blacksmith in tow. Demand was still so high during this time that when signing treaties with the Native Americans, the United States government was forced to include a clause which provided the tribes with access to the blacksmith embedded at every Army fort.

As a need for their services continued to decline, blacksmithing became more synonymous with farriery. That is, of course, until the introduction of the automobile at which point many blacksmiths surrendered to the times and became the world's first auto mechanics. Interest in the trade continued to drop with perhaps the lowest point coming during the 1960s when few if any new blacksmiths were taking up the trade.

This changed in the 1970s as a growing trend in self-sufficiency saw renewed interest in the craft, albeit in more of an amateur capacity. 1973 also saw the creation of the Artist Blacksmith Association of North America, with 27 founding members. As of 2013, that number has grown to more than 4,000. Additional branches can be found around the world with the British chapter forming in 1978. Many other parts of the world never saw a noted decrease in the number of blacksmiths, and their smiths continue to do what they have always done, repair and create tools made of steel and iron for their local communities.

Common Terms

Iron: This element occurs naturally in the environment, though almost never in a pure form. It typically contains impurities including most commonly sulfide and oxide. Steel with a low amount of carbon, wrought iron and other soft variations of iron are all typically referred to simply as iron.

Wrought iron: This type of iron is almost completely pure as its impurities have been removed. It contains very little carbon by weight, usually around .04 percent.

Steel: Steel is made up of iron mixed more carbon than regular iron (up to 1.7 percent). This carbon provides the blacksmith with the ability to determine how hard or malleable the end product ultimately turns out to be. The more carbon the steel contains the harder it ultimately becomes.

Cast iron: This type of iron contains by weight at least 2 percent and ultimately up to 6 percent carbon. This excess of carbon makes cast iron more brittle than either natural iron or steel. It is impossible to forge cast iron without first changing it to a more malleable form of iron.

CHAPTER 1

Basic Tools

To begin practicing the art of blacksmithing, you are going to need at least 5 basic things. Something to heat the metal you are working with, something to hold the metal you are working with, somewhere to put the piece of metal you are working on, something to work on the piece of metal with and a way to cool the piece of metal when you are done with it.

Forge

A blacksmith is only as good as their forge which is why a variety of forge types are discussed in chapter 3. Regardless of the specifics, all forges contain the same basic parts, something to provide fuel for a fire and a way to manipulate the air in the forge to increase the heat. Forges using coke (a variant of coal) and a bellows were common once upon a time, now propane forges which use fans for air are the most common type employed by amateur blacksmiths working from homemade forges. A propane forge provides novice smiths with a greater degree of control than more traditional methods. An acetylene torch needs to generate at least 40,000 BTUs to be a viable blacksmithing tool.

Tongs

A set of tongs is vital for the aspiring blacksmith as it provides the primary way for holding extremely hot metal. It is important to invest in a set of tongs as they vary in size from those that hold tiny wires to those large enough to hold pieces of metal that weigh a ton or more. With that in mind, when starting out you can generally get by with a set of flat jawed tongs, a pair of pick-up tongs for use in jobs which require tempering, and a mixed use pair of tongs for working with round or square iron pieces. Vices and clamps are also used depending on the work.

When using tongs, it is important to always ensure they take ahold of what you are working with in the proper way. When they are holding on to something for maximum control and effectiveness the jaws of the tongs must be touching the metal across its full circumference with almost no space (but still a little space) between them. Tongs are refitted each time they are used. To do so, heat the jaws until they turn red, place the piece of metal between them, then hammer the tongs so they are holding the piece of metal correctly. It is crucial to never use tongs that are too small or too big as doing so can lead to accidents and serious injury.

Anvil

The anvil you use needs to be strong enough to absorb countless blows from a substantial hammer. Anvils come in a variety of shapes and sizes, the most common shape for blacksmiths being one that contains a set of two holes, known as the a pritchel hole and a hardie hole. The pritchel hole is used when the blacksmith needs to put a hole in a piece of metal as it holds the slug which is pushed through the metal to prevent it from creating distorted holes. The hardie hole holds the tools which are used to do things like bending or curving metal or putting edges on things.

Modern blacksmithing anvils typically are forged of cast iron before a steel layer is welded on for increase strength. It is important to place your anvil on a thick piece of wood which is sunk a few feet into the ground and then firmly attached the anvil to the wood in an effort to mitigate unwanted vibrations. A good blacksmithing anvil should weigh around 300 pounds to hold up to the stresses it will be placed under.

Hammers

Much like with tongs, you will need a variety of hammers depending on the work you are doing. The most important is the ball-peen, the type of hammer that has a flat head at one end and a ball on the other. They weight of the hammer should be enough that it provides plenty of results compared with your level of exertion but not one that is so heavy that you become tired while lifting it too quickly.

For most people this will be a hammer that is around 1.5 to 2 pounds, though heavy hammers should be considered depending on your overall level of fitness. For blacksmithing purposes, a 4-pound hammer is considered the standard and working up to one should be your goal if you plan on sticking with blacksmithing for an extended period of time.

Quench Tub

Once you are done working with a piece of metal that is red hot, you will need a place to put it so that it cools off as quickly as possible. That's where a quench tub comes in and it is the last thing you need before you get started pounding on metal for yourself. A water storage drum that is at least 55-gallons will work well for most people, though again, it is important to take into consideration the types of work you will be performing most often when it comes to specifics. This water can also be used to control forge flames that become unruly without sacrificing too much fuel.

CHAPTER 2

Basics of the Forge

Whenever you start a project, no matter what that project is, you have to have a certain measure of is that you need to have the proper tools. And when it comes to blacksmithing those tools undoubtedly will be the forge, the anvil and the hammer. Probably the most iconic part of any blacksmith shop is the hammer. In TV and movies the blacksmith hammer has sometimes been exaggerated to gargantuan proportions but you don't need to have the hammering power of a mythic Greek god like Prometheus in order to be a blacksmith, for all practical purposes you will just need a good 2 pound hammer to get the job done.

From all accounts the first prototype of the hammer was the human fist. The pounding motion of the hammer is just reproducing the pounding that a human fist would produce, except the hammer fist of course, is able to withstand the heat of the forge. The traditional Blacksmiths' hammer is available at most hardware stores and you can of course order them online through major online platforms such as amazon.com.

The most useful hammer you will come across will always be the "cross peen" hammer. The cross peen hammer is used to draw out the steel while the flat end of the same hammer has an octagonal face and is used to create circular indentations. The heavier hammers are always what are known as "sledge hammers" and are for truly heavy stock that needs to be forged.

And speaking of the forge, if you are just beginning you are probably wondering what forges are even about. Basically cauldrons of immense heat, they can come in many shapes and styles. The traditional hand-cranked, air blowing blacksmith forge can still be found at most hardware stores.

If you can't buy one however, you can easily make one yourself with just a few basic materials. And at the most basic level all you need is a basin that can hold enough coal to sustain the melting point of steel. The forge will also need an air flow of some sort, this is usually accomplished through centrifugally fanned air entering from below. This fan is used to control the overall temperature of the forge, creating less or more heat through the blowing of the fan upon the coals.

The two main options that you have when it comes to a fan is whether or not it is going to be hand driven or machine driven. When use a hand cranked fan it immediately stops when you take your hand off of it, but if you use an electric fan it is usually controlled by some sort of foot pedal, allowing you to turn it on and off by stepping on a switch. Being able to control when the heat of the forge is turned on or off is, of course, of extreme importance.

Proper maintenance of a forge includes keeping up a medium sized fire at all time, not too big, and not too small, just keep up the standard status quo. In doing this you have to keep in mind that each and every previous fire that was in your forge was bound to have created a remnant of what is termed "coke" (not to be confused with coca cola or the illicit street drug of the same name!) Coke is essentially the remains of the previous day's coal, usually smile cinders or ashes that are left behind in the forge.

These small remnants are important to note, because their remains should generate a healthy blue flame for your forge, this is a clear indication and go ahead to you that you will have a clean fire. If for whatever reason there are other undesired elements mixed in with the coke in your forge, the flame may turn a sickly yellow and give off a rather acrid odor; this is a clear indication that you may have a dirty fire on your hands. This means that you need to clean the forge out of unwanted elements so that they don't corrupt the composition of the steel that you are trying to forge.

A standout feature of some of the more modern forges is the utilization of a screening apparatus that prevents most of these contaminants from breaking through in the first place. Known as a "hinging smoke catcher" these devices are similar to catalytic converters in cars, in the way that they filter and purify emissions from the forger. Because once you have these installed, smoke emissions are mixed with the surrounding oxygen when you start up the fire and then fed back into the catcher cleaning out the air. Implementing this smoke catcher will allow you to have a fairly smokeless fire.

When you light your fire make sure that you allow for a little bit of a draft and throw some wood chips into the coke mixture of your forge, mix it around, rake it up, and set it ablaze. Let this mixture burn well and then push it up into the center and add what is termed "green coal" to the mixture; green coal is essentially wet coal. This wet coal helps to further facilitate the flame as the green coal turns to coke just keep pushing it in and adding more green coal to the edges until you have a blazing fire.

With your fire blazing the next thing you need to do is set up your anvil, this is where you metal will be shaped and molded. Anvils are a bit hard to come by nowadays, and sometimes you may have to make a special order to receive them, but we will discuss some of the finer aspects of acquisition a bit further in the next chapter.

Once you have your anvil in place you are going to want to secure it with either bolts or spikes on a block of wood. The basic anvil has 6 main parts; the horn, the face, the body, the tool hole, the round or pritchel hole, and the base of horn. This is the classic anvil shape although your model may vary.

You should try to engineer the whole thing so that with your anvil sitting on top of the block of wood the height of the whole apparatus should have your fingers able to touch the top of the anvil while standing up straight and arms hanging freely. This kind of setup allows you to have the right kind of range to employ full length arm strokes as you strike your hammer on the anvil. These three elements, hammer, anvil and fire are the basics of the forge.

CHAPTER 3

Types of Forges

Over the past 100 years, fuels like acetylene, natural gas and others have become more widely used then coal, though charcoal is still considered the gold standard for a master blacksmith. If you decide to use a natural gas forge it is important to take special care when heating steel as if it is done improperly it can leave too much carbon in the steel. Natural gas heats carbon to the point where it vaporizes, making it easy for it to seep into steel that is being worked.

Build a forge

There are a wide variety of forges you can choose from when it comes to setting up your own personal workshop. What follows are a list of things to consider when building the forge that is right for you.

- **Decide what you will be working with:** If you plan on working with iron or steel you will need a forge that reaches anywhere from 1200 degrees Fahrenheit to 2550 degrees Fahrenheit, metals like bronze or brass can be worked at cooler temperatures.

- **Choose a fuel**: Propane, liquefied propane and natural gas are all readily available fuels that you can use without worrying about the ventilation requirements that charcoal or coal require. Remember, natural gasses provide heat which is easier to control for novice blacksmiths.

- **Consider what you will be working on most frequently**: Most hobby grade blacksmiths will be able to work from a small pit, those who want to create items that are the size of a longsword or larger should consider a forge that is wider and longer and those interested in creating very large items should consider a forge which includes an overhead hoist. Hearth-size forges are appropriate for beginners and will be discussed in detail below.

- **Decide on placement**: A forge placed in an enclosed workshop is more protected from the elements but it will require additional considerations when it comes to mitigating heat. Most hobby grade blacksmiths have their needs adequately met by an outdoor forge.

Charcoal Forge

- Dig a foundation that is at least 3.5 inches deep with a circumference of at least 1 foot.

- Ensure the top of your foundation is level before adding reinforcements around the sides and add concrete to the form you created.

- Add 2 feet of bricks to the outside of the foundation while leaving the insides empty. Ensure you leave an opening at the front to add in metal and an opening at the back to get rid of ashes and add in charcoal. The removal space should be about one foot by one foot with the entrance hole sized based on your needs.

- A third opening needs to be left to allow for an air supply, regardless of what type of air supply you are planning on, a cast iron pipe with a circumference of 4 inches should be adequate for your needs.

- Add a liner or metal pan to the inside of your forge, a stainless steel option that is at least .25 inches thick and 3.5 inches deep should suffice for most purposes. There should be a hole in the center to take air flow into account.

- Add a floor to your forge above the liner which is also made of brick. The floor should form a flat space for you to place items on top of. Try and center the flat space at a level which is easy for you to reach.

- Cover the top of the forge.

- Connect your air supply, add two handfuls of charcoal and you are ready to heat your metal. Always turn on your air supply after adding the charcoal.

Coal Forge

- Take a metal square that is 8 inches squared and drill a number of holes into it in an area that is 1-inch x 1.5 inches.

- Take a pipe with a 2-inch circumference and ensure that it is roughly 7 inches long. Weld this pipe into place below the area you drilled holes into.

- Place a small piece of metal on top of the holes to serve as a lid.

- Take 4 reinforced metal legs and weld them to the four corners of the square before adding supports between them to maintain stability.

- Cut a hole in the pipe that fits the type of air supply you are planning to use. Attach the secondary pipe so that it points towards the sky.

- The first pipe is used for an ash trap and the second is for the air supply.

- Take a brake drum (unused) and set it on top of the forge so that it lines up with the ash trap holes before cutting holes into it so it can reach the ash trap below.

- Weld the brake drum into place and use it to hold the coal you will use to warm the metal you will be working with.

Propane Forge

- Decide on the number of burners your forge will use, this forge must be built outside.

- A gas forge has two main parts, the body and the burners. The body can be comprised of any metal container, depending on the size of the metal you will be working with.

- After choosing a metal container that can withstand high temperatures, line it with insulation. Firebrick insulation is an easy and cheap solution that isn't terribly efficient, while ceramic insulation is quite good at what it does and is equally expensive.

- Depending on the size of your forge, consider purchasing propane burners or, for smaller forges, a torch can be used (40,000 BTUs recommended)

- Weld the appropriate parts onto the metal container to utilize the propane and ensure the excess gas can be vented.

- Ensure your container has a sturdy, airtight door.

- Place the container on a stand which allows for it to be moved easily while remaining strong and resistant to the heat. Do not keep excess fuel nearby while in use.

- Always be cautious when using propane as a fuel source, never light the forge at the air choke point, always use a long match or torch and light it from the front.

CHAPTER 4

Stance and Technique

Proper stance in the forge is needed in order to be able to make each hammer blow as effective as you possibly can. Developing a good hammer technique is something that comes with time and it may take a few go rounds in order for you to develop a good technique. After plenty of repetition however, it will soon become automatic. The first key to developing a good stance is in the way that you stand.

You need to stand at the anvil with your legs spread far enough apart so that you can brace yourself firmly with your center of gravity. In doing this always try to keep one foot a little bit back while your other foot is pushed forward directly under the anvil. You should also try to make sure that you bend your head directly over the anvil as much as possible with you head tilted slightly to the side so that you will be able to ensure that your hammer will be able to safely swing past when you deliver your hammer blows.

This is very important for your own safety since it is incredibly easy to make a miscalculation and have the hammer bounce back in your own direction and cause you serious injury. So keep your head safely tilted away from any kind of blowback but yet still close enough in range that you can overlook your work in fairly fine detail and have a clear view of the work that is being done to the hot metal on the anvil giving you sufficient enough knowledge to now where to you should direct your next hammer blow.

Along with making sure you don't get wacked in the head with your own hammer you should also be careful not to let any flaming debris from the forge, whether its cinders or ash dust, fly back into your eyes.

Traditionally this is the reason why most Blacksmiths always squint their eyes in order to prevent an eyeful of burning hot ash from coming their way. This method may seem a bit crude, but squinting the eyes usually works to deter most debris, if however you wish for more substantial safety a pair of welder's goggles would do just fine.

Proper maintenance of tools is another must when it comes to implementing proper blacksmith technique. And most importantly in this is the upkeep of your hammer's facing. A hammer that is used on a regular basis needs to be routinely dressed in order to keep the face (the part of the tool that is pounding into the anvil) in good working order. So let's make sure that you are up on the proper dressing technique for this kind of hammer facing.

The first thing that you need to do is open up the middle of the fire and fill it up with a bunch of charcoal and use the mineral coal in this instance only as a backer. Once this is accomplished be sure to heat only the face that needs to be dressed so that you do not change the shape or inadvertently disturb the eye. After doing this you need to put the hammer in a nice pile of dust, neatly tucked away in the forge to let it cool.

When using your hammer the most important thing to know is that the hammer is angled backward and the first motion will always be from the contraction of the fingers. This will give the hammer its initial movement; this is then immediately followed up by the arching pattern of the arm until the hammer strikes upon the anvil. It is then a simple matter of mathematics as the rest of the muscles of your body follow that initial movement and the force will soon multiply itself exponentially as you beat the metal into shape.

And when it comes to beating up your metal into appropriate forms you should know some of the terminology involved in the process. One of the most frequent terms you will hear when it comes to blacksmith technique will undoubtedly be "upsetting". Although in common parlance, being "upset" means you are having an emotional problem, in blacksmithing "upsetting" us simply referencing the technique of pushing metals together and making a piece shorter and thicker. Basically it's the same concept of kneading clay or dough, it's just that instead of shaping the material with your hands you are using the heat, anvil and hammer to mold the clay of your steel into the shapes that you desire. Once you master these basic techniques and procedures you will be well on your way to having a fit little smith shop.

CHAPTER 5

Knife Making Techniques

There is many people interested in learning how to make a knife with their own two hands. But like anything you must take the time to learn the process properly. In this guide I will try and offer you easy steps to follow that will guide you properly on how to make a good knife. If your knife does not turn out on the first try, don't give up just remember practice makes perfect. Below are eight steps that will help you to build a durable knife.

Step 1: Design the blade of Your Knife

The first thing you need to do is to draw a sketch of your knife on a piece of graph paper. Just like you would need architectural drawings of a building before you built it, the same holds true when you are designing a knife. When you have finally come up with the desired shape or design of your knife it will put you in a better position to get the desired form that you seek for your knife.

Banana shapes are the most traditional shapes for knives that you will see. But you can make your knife into any shape that you like. Come up with an amazing design for your knife with your drawings. Make sure that you also include the shape of your handle in your drawings. The most comfortable handles will be the most easiest to carry and handle. At this first stage of the design also decide how you will attach the handle to the blade. The easiest way to accomplish this is to join it via full tang.

Step 2: Choose materials for your knife

Choosing good materials for your knife is crucial in producing a knife that is going to work for you for a long time. Don't waste time choosing material that is inferior quality. Experts will advise you to choose carbon steel instead of stainless steel for the blade.

Stainless steel will not make a fine blade. Once you have chosen the material that you wish to use for your blade, it is then time to choose material that will be suitable for the handle of your knife. There are several materials that you may consider using for your knife handle such as leather, wood, metal, gems, stones etc. If you are looking for a handle that is going to be durable and strong, make sure you shop around and obtain your material at a very low price. You will also need some epoxy and pins.

Step 3: Cut the blade roughly

At this point you need to cut the blade roughly. In order to accomplish this process you will need certain tools such as an angle grinder, files, vise, drill and hacksaw. You will also need to get some safety accessories such as jacket to avoid sparks, safety glasses, work gloves.

If the material is thick for your blade use a hacksaw, if it is thin, use a jewelers saw. Now you need to place your blade in a vise and start grinding it. You can use a hard wheel or stone wheel for this purpose. Put it in on an angle so that you can cut away excess metal. Use a flap wheel to grind the edge of your blade. When you have completed this step then drill some rivet holes of appropriate size.

Whenever you are making a first cut make sure that it is a rough one. This means instead of cutting the blade in its original shape cut it in a rectangular shape, this will leave lots of metal around the blade.

Step 4: Perform finishing

In order to obtain a proper finish on your knife there is certain measures that must be taken. For instance these will include: sandpaper, grits, and sanding block. You can use a power drill or a sanding wheel.

Take your design for your knife that you have sketched and mark out your blade. You will have to follow the patterns on the knife blade, make sure that you use good files because bad files could ruin your blade.

Step 5: Heating

Once you have finished the sanding of your knife the next thing to do is to give your blade a heat treatment. For this purpose you may use a gas forge, torch, or coal forge. During this heating process there are further steps that include hardening and tempering the blade.

You need to heat the blade then quench it so that it may become extremely hard. In the latter step tempering, heat the knife to a lower temperature to make the knife less brittle.

Now you must get a hardening bath so that you can quench the metal. There are several methods to do it such as quenching with oil, water, or air. You may also need a magnet to determine the hardening temperature. Then make a fire and heat the blade in medium high orange heat. Heat the knife until it becomes nonmagnetic.

Step 6: Second Finishing

Perform the finishing step that you just did for a second time. This time you are likely to go to a higher grit. At this point you should also try to get the scale. After this polish the blade. For polishing you will need a polishing wheel, bench grinder, and black polishing material.

Step 7: Fix handle

Once you have finished the blade it is time to get a grip for you knife. Use the material that you have bought for this purpose. Use rivet and some sticking material for this purpose.

Step 8: Get a proper edge for your knife

In this step you want to get a proper sharp edge for your knife. Use a sharpening stone to accomplish this task. These simple eight steps can help guide you to make an amazing knife for yourself.

These steps will help guide you to building a simple beginners knife.

CHAPTER 6

Some Basic Projects
for Beginner Blacksmith

Steel forging

Materials:

- Anvil

- Ceramic wool (1 inch thick)

- Coffee can

- Firebricks

- Hammer

- Metal strips

- Propane torch

Instructions:

The first step of this project relates to the picking of the Torch. You will need to get a propane torch which possesses a permanent button with ON instructions. This button is necessary for efficient working so that you may not need to permanently hold up the button for the supply of gas. It will not be possible while you will be using a forge. In the picture, you can see that the red button acts like a trigger, whereas the little metal button enables the locking of the trigger to enable permanent ON position.

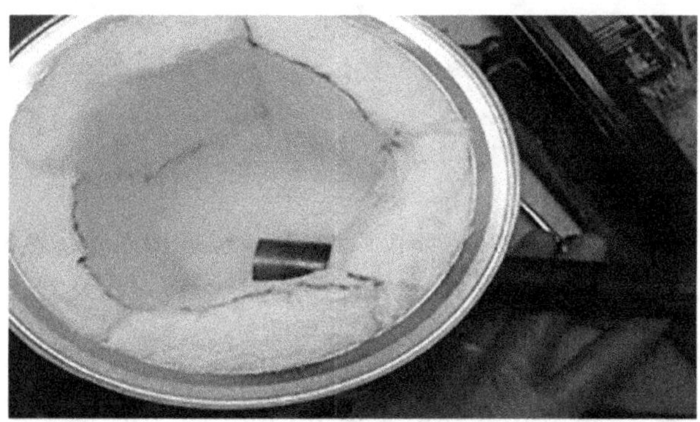

The next step is to prepare the selected Can. Strip off any paint or plastic from the outer portion of the coffee can. Use a drill machine and make a hole at the side. The hole should be according to the nozzle of the torch so that it can fit into the hole easily.

Now treat the ceramic wool and cut it to a length which is suitable for covering the inside of the can. For covering the far end of the can a separate piece of ceramic wool will be needed. When the entire can is covered with the wool, the shape must be kept in a natural form without ant fasteners or adhesive. Now make a hole in the wool, right in front of the hole which you made for the nozzle.

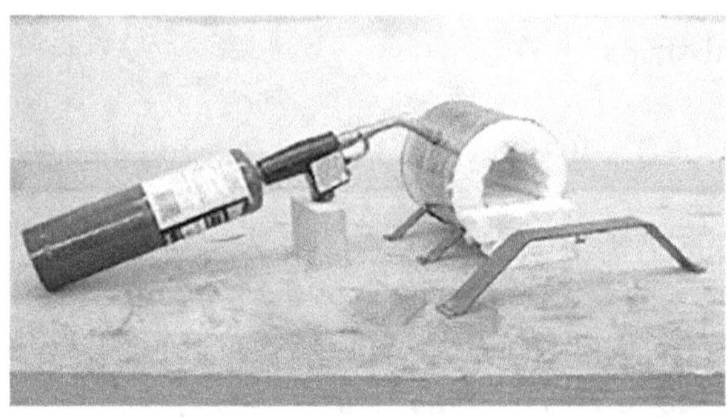

Now make a base. You can continue with forging at this step as well but it is necessary to build a stand for the can so that the heated can may not distort or harm any of the table or chairs.

Based upon the particular angle at which the torch will be placed, you will adjust the base for the torch so that the hole at the can faces the nozzle without distortion.

The firebricks will provide a rough solid surface for keeping the metals on fire during the heat supply. Firebricks also aid in covering the gap at the front portion of the can so that content heat is provided. Now light up the torch and put the email object for forging. After successive heating sessions, use tongs to remove the metal. Place the heated metal over some hard surface. You can use a real anvil or concrete rock me which will work out great. Now strike the metal several times for making any of the desired shapes.

Dinner bells triangle

Materials:

- Rebar- 3 feet

- Iron piece- 1 feet

- Heating torch

- anvil

- Gloves

Instructions:

This project is suitable for homes as well as for hostels or other areas where the inhabitants live in rooms located within eh vicinity of the home in such a way that calling them for dinner or another meal is quite hard. So this dinner bell triangle can be used to gather all of them for a meal.

The major portion of this project comprises of a piece of rebar which was around 3 feet in measurement lengthwise. You will also need a side piece for around 1 foot to make the striking bar. The striking bar will be having an attached handle, to ring the bell.

In this project using rebar is the most cost friendly way of completing the project, but the sound produced by rebar is not that shrill. But it is enough if the house or hostel is not too big. However, you can make alterations as needed if you have some other material around.

First of all divide rebar into 3 equal portions, along its length. Next steps to heat up these portions in such a way that two points are bent together to form the triangle. In order to give a clearer idea consider that of the rebar is 36 inches in length, you will be make two lines with chalk at two points. One will be at 12 inches and the next will be at a point of 24 inches. These points will make three quail portion for the bar. For heating, the bar follows the lines drawn. Proceed with bending the bar. You will just give it a shape of triangle but will not continue with closing the triangle.

Now use a smaller piece of stock to make up the hoop. The bar will hang to this hoop it will hang by. In the case of the hop you can carry on welding, to form the triangle. An alternative is to hook the hoop along the open side of the triangle. Anvil will be used to make this hoop.

Next, you will go for making the handle of the bell. Turn down a pine to get a cylindrical structure. Make some groves by turning it down. You can add up the color to make the handle brighter and attractive. Run the lathe with a low speed to make a mark with crayons and use a torch for heating up and melting the crayons.

Chain mail

Materials:

- Steel wire- 14 gauge

- Springs

- Wooden boards

- Drill machine

- Bolt cutter

Instructions:

The Term "Chainmail" used for the past days Ring Mail". It is regarded as both an armor as well as fabric. During the first part of this project, you will use the springs to cut out the rings. Spinning f these springs will result in cutting of the wire.

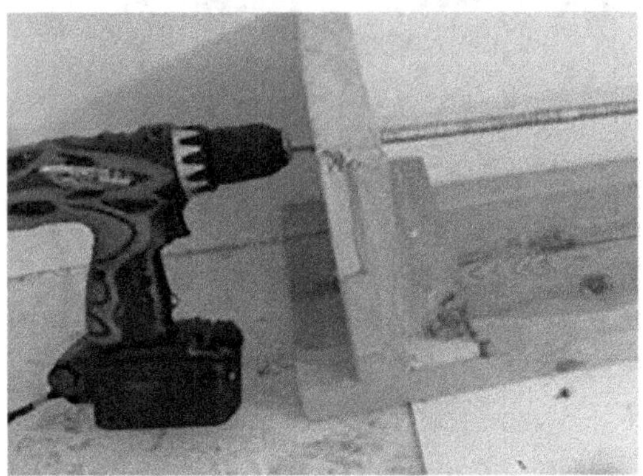

You will make the springs by constructing a little jig by applying wood scraps of wood. You will use a rod with 36 inches in length rod and 3/8 inch in width. Now two holes will be drilled in order to provide space for rotation of the rod.

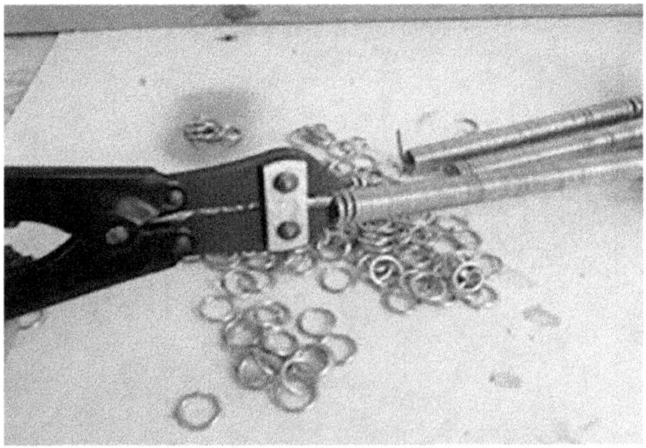

Now spin the coils by applying a drill with a variable. The coiled wire will end up in a fine form. When the springs are completed, the next step is cutting up the coils. You will use an 8 inches bolt cutter pair. Large bolt cutters will not allow for snipping up the rings. Cut a lot of rings in the same way. These will be then weaved together to make up the whole fabric.

Chainmail gloves

Specifications:

- Weight will be 600g

- Steel rings - 3141

- Ring - 7mm diameter

- Steel wire - 69m

- Ammonia- 500 ml

- Oil- few drops

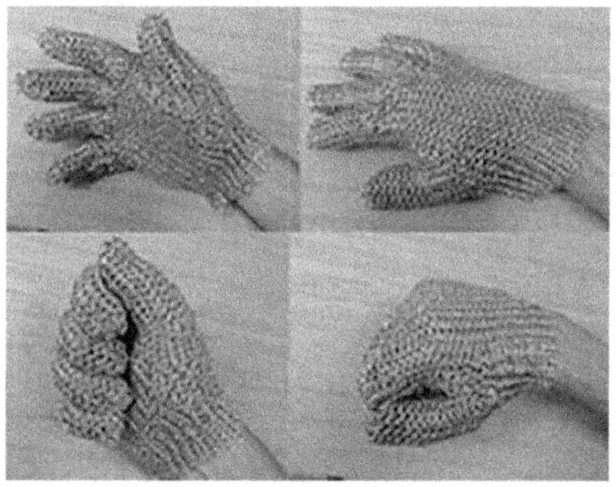

Instructions:

Make up a chain mail as described in the last project in a square shape, in such a way that it can wrap your finger. Make it a little tighter for the fingers as the connecting rings will make the circumference of the fingers larger. Weave the pattern along the length of the fingers.

When the weaving of fingers will be completed, you will start connecting these fingers tighter. Fit these over the hand in a position with a natural fit and they start deciding about the direction of the connection. Keep connecting to a point where there is a one ring space at the top and bottom portion. Once the middle and index finger will be connected, the middle finger will turn into a twist. Hence, it is necessary that you use 2 rings for linking the fingers and move on by repeating this link.

Before linking the thumb you will add a group of chainmail for the length of the pinky fingers. The weaving of rings will be continued in the same way. The last step for the project is to give a final touch to the glove. For this, you may use any of the bleaching agents like ammonia. Take 500ml of ammonia and soak the woven gloves in that liquid for at least 2 hours. Continue rubbing the glove while it is still in the liquid. Now take it off for the liquid and let it get dry in sunlight. Now use any oil to rub over the whole surface and leave it sunlight for 12 hours.

CHAPTER 7

Easy Knife Making

Pocketknife is a very important tool and most of the survivalists also love to use it. The reason is that it's easy to carry and it can easily fit in the pocket. Moreover its unique design make it safe as well.

There are two important things about the pocketknife. These are its blade and handle. It is designed in a way that you can fold it easily. When you don't need it, just fold and keep it in the pocket. Here the aim of this chapter is to make it easy for you to learn the DIY project to design a pocketknife. You can design your pocket knife in any shape that you want. And remember its size always remain small.

Some tools and Materials:

To make a pocketknife some simple tools are used that are easily available at your home. If they are not available, you can get them from a store. Without any difficulty you will get all the materials required just from a single shop.

The materials needs are: wood saw, metal saw, piece of metal, wood, bolts and nuts, PVC and drill. The metal will be used to make a blade while the PVC will be used along with bolts and wood to make a beautiful handle for your pocket knife. Moreover you will also need a metal cutter to cut the blade properly.

Whenever you start your project of making knife, make sure that you are using some safety equipment as well. These may include safety glasses, gloves, shoes and jacket. These safety measures will help you to stay away from the sparks and other dangers.

Build the pocketknife:

To build a pocketknife demands much patience. First make sure that you have all the materials required. Without the materials, you would not be able to make proper pocketknife for yourself.

First of all you will make a PVC handle for your pocket knife. To make this handle, cut the PVP pipe horizontally all the way through the other side. Now it's time to flatten the PVC pipe by heating. Heat it and turn in square shape. You can use any material for heating purpose such as heat gun or any other such element. But remember that it should turn the PVC pipe in some proper square shape. Don't heat too much that it losses its shape. After the next step you will use this PVC to make handle.

Now prepare the metal blade for your pocketknife. For this purpose you need a piece of metal. Draw the desired shape of blade on it. Now pick up some saw or metal cutter to cut it properly. You are free to choose any design or shape for your metal blade. But make sure that it is designed in a way that it will meet your needs longer.

Assemble the parts of pocketknife:

When you are done with the handle and blade of your pocketknife, its time to assemble them together. For appropriate assembling you requisite to drill the hole in the PVC and the metal as well.

Make sure that the holes are properly aligned and of the same size of the bolts. First put the top bolt and secure it with a nut. Now put the second bolt downward and secure it with the nut. Drill another half hole near to the top hole just to make a perfect grip.

Now cut the wood of the size of the handle to make it more secure. This step is not important but if you perform it, you will get an aesthetic pleasing look for your pocketknife. Secure this wood with some bolts.

After that, use some stone or a file to make your knife sharp. Without sharpening you will not get the desired results.

In short, the above mentioned few steps will help you to make a beautiful pocketknife. You can use this pocketknife anywhere you want. It will serve many purposes for your survival as well. As it's easy to carry, people love to take it with themselves anywhere when they feel any threat or danger. Always keep your pocketknife sharp so that you may work with it even in some emergency situation.

In the previous three chapters you learned to make pocketknife, simple knife and a survival knife. Now here you are going to learn how to make a hunting knife. This knife is larger than the survival knife.

It can be used for hunting and as a best weapon. It's also not very difficult to build. By using some simple tools you can make it easily. People often use this hunting knife for survival.

Materials and Tools needed to make a hunting knife:

To make hunting knife same materials are required as you used to make a pocketknife. These materials are sandpaper, drill, wood, metal piece, heating material, pairs of 4-5 bolts and nuts and so on.

You can use wood or bone to make the handle of the hunting knife. But try to get some thicker wooden piece because the hunting knife needs to be very strong compared to the pocketknife. The thicker wooden handle or any other such material will hold the metal blade properly and keep it safe as well.

Blade of hunting knife:

When deciding about the hunting knife, a very important factor to be considered is its blade. The size of the hunting blade should be appropriate. As the too big hunting knives have some law prohibitions.

Carrying too big knife can put you in some trouble. Moreover, very small knife would not be able to serve different hunting purposes. So build a blade of medium size or an average size that is easily available in the market. You can also create teeth on the other side of the blade. In this way you would be able to use it in more appropriate way.

Apart from this, keep your hunting knife a light weight and durable. First draw the shape of the hunting knife on some metal and with the help of metal cutter, cut it. Unlike pocketknife, you are not free to design any shape for the hunting knife. These knifes usually come in certain shapes and designs to serve the hunting purpose. So never mess up with some complicated designs. After cutting the blade, if there are some imperfections that you notice then its time style it smooth.

Handle of the hunting knife:

Handle of the hunting knife is as important as its material is. You can use any material for this purpose but wood is the best option for the beginners. Drill four holes, two at the top of the handle and 2 at the bottom so that you may get a firm grip. Moreover drill the holes of certain sizes just equal to size of rivets.

Assemble the parts of hunting knife:

After designing the blade and handle of your hunting knife, make some efforts to assemble the parts of hunting knife. For this purpose grab the blade and fix the pieces of wood directly on top of each other. Now use the bolts to secure them. When you are done with it, take some file or any other material to sharpen the blade.

In this way you can make an amazing hunting knife that will serve several important functions for you.

Simple Metal knife

Materials:

- Anvil

- Hammer

- Metal strips

- Wooden handle

- Nails

Instructions:

The steel piece used for making the knife will be hammered again and again so that it can make up a good position. The continuous hammering along the side of the metal piece is the most crucial step for making up the knife. It is usually regarded as squashing of the metal.

The squashing results in making the edges of the metal thicker around the edges. The central portion of the metal piece will remain of the same thickness with which you started. Once squashing will be completed you will start with flattening of the metal piece in such a way that you will lay it out anvil and will flatten it out.

In order to attain the inner curve of the knife, you will need to continue with offset hammering. The side of the hammering that is affected. The side alongside the anvil will also be worked upon at the similar time. So hammering comes to be the most important task for enabling perfect curves out of the metal piece.

Make accurate use of the anvil surface and the horn. The next step will be to dig the curve between the handle and the metal. For making that space you will continue with half face hammering. For this step, you will put the metal for knife half way over the anvil. The rim of the anvil will be located where you want the placement of the drop coil. The blade part will be hanging across the anvil. The handle of the knife will lie over the anvil.

It will be done without finishing the surface of the blade. Hammering will enable you to get the exact shape of the knife. It will enable you to make a distinct drop.

Hatchet

Materials:

- Anvil

- Firebricks

- Hammer

- Metal strips

- Propane torch

Instructions:

You will need to get a propane torch which possesses a permanent button with power instructions. This button is necessary for efficient working so that you may not need to permanently hold up the button for the supply of gas. It will not be possible while you will be using a forge. In the picture, you can see that the red button acts like a trigger, whereas the little metal button enables the locking of the trigger to enable permanent power position.

The next step is to prepare the selected Can. Strip off any paint or plastic from the outer portion of the coffee can. Use a drill machine and make a hole at the side. The hole should be according to the nozzle of the torch so that it can fit into the hole easily.

Now treat the hammer and cut it to a length which is suitable for covering the inside of the can. For covering the far end of the can a separate piece of the ceramic hammer will be needed. When the entire can is covered with the hammer, the shape must be kept in a natural form without ant fasteners or adhesive. Now make a hole within the hammer, right in front of the hole which you made for the nozzle.

Now make a base. You can continue with forging at this step as well but it is necessary to build a stand for the can so that the heated can may not distort or harm any of the table or chairs.

Tool For Curving Pumpkin

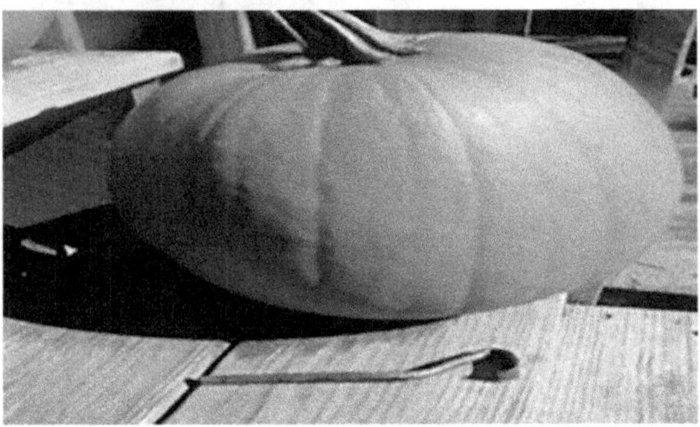

Materials:

- Iron rod

- Twisting tongs

- Drill

- Heating torch

Instructions:

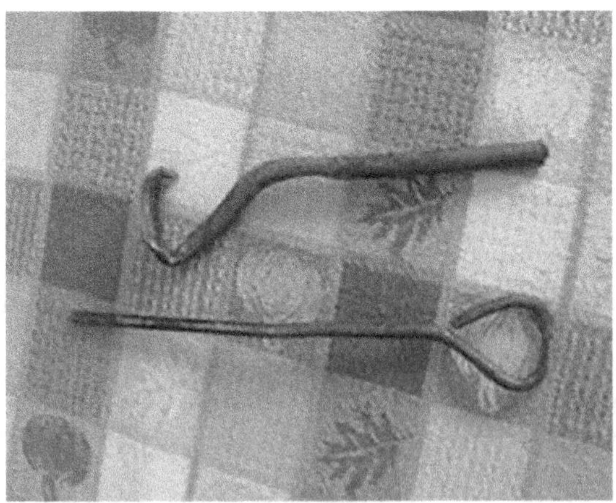

The steel piece used for making this tool it will be hammered again and again so that it can make up a good position. The continuous hammering along the side of the metal piece is the most crucial step for making up the knife. It is usually regarded as squashing of the metal.

The squashing results in making the edges of the metal thicker around the edges. The central portion of the metal piece will remain of the same thickness with which you started. Once squashing will be completed you will start with flattening of the metal piece in such a way that you will lay it out anvil and will flatten it out.

In order to attain the inner curve of the knife, you will need to continue with offset hammering. The side of the hammering that is affected. The side alongside the anvil will also be worked upon at the similar time. So hammering comes to be the most important task for enabling perfect curves out of the metal piece.

Make accurate use of the anvil surface and the horn. The next step will be to dig the curve between the handle and the metal. For making that space you will continue with half face hammering. For this step, you will put the metal for knife half way over the anvil.

Pritcher-hole clamp

Materials:

- Anvil

- Hammer

- Metal strips

- Wooden handle

- Nails

Instructions:

The major portion of this project comprises of a piece of rebar which was around 3 feet in measurement lengthwise. You will also need a side piece for around 1 foot to make the striking bar. The striking bar will be having an attached handle, to ring the bell.

In this project using rebar is the most cost friendly way of completing the project, but the sound produced by rebar is not that shrill. But it is enough if the house or hostel is not too big. However, you can make alterations as needed if you have some other material around.

First of all divide rebar into 3 equal portions, along its length. Next steps to heat up these portions in such a way that two points are bent together to form the triangle. In order to give a clearer idea consider that of the rebar is 36 inches in length, you will be make two lines with chalk at two points.

One will be at 12 inches and the next will be at a point of 24 inches. These points will make three quail portion for the bar. For heating, the bar follows the lines drawn. Proceed with bending the bar. You will just give it a shape of triangle but will not continue with closing the triangle.

In order to attain the inner curve, you will need to continue with offset hammering. The side of the hammering that is affected. The side alongside the anvil will also be worked upon at the similar time. So hammering comes to be the most important task for enabling perfect curves out of the metal piece.

Make accurate use of the anvil surface and the horn. The next step will be to dig the curve between the handle and the metal. For making that space you will continue with half face hammering. For this step, you will put the metal for knife half way over the anvil. The rim of the anvil will be located where you want the placement of the drop coil. The blade part will be hanging across the anvil. The handle of the knife will lie over the anvil.

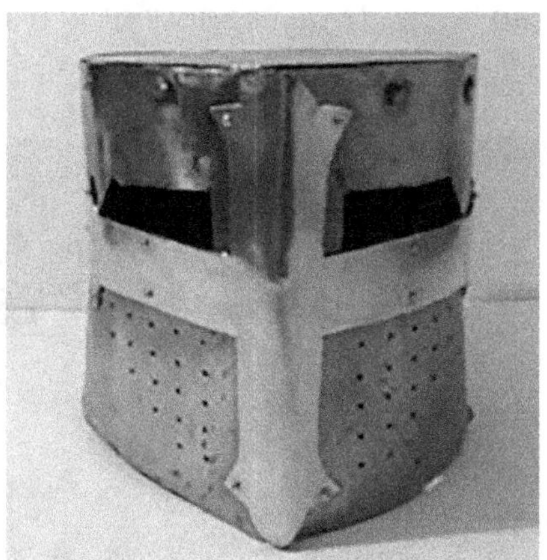

Medieval Helm

Materials:

- Sheet steel -18 gauge

- Forging setup

- Hand tools

- A sheet metal shear

- Hand shears

- Jigsaw

- Drill

- Rivets

- Wire brush

- Emory paper

Instructions:

This steel helmet can be made in a variety of ways. It can be sued as an armor as well as a decoration piece.

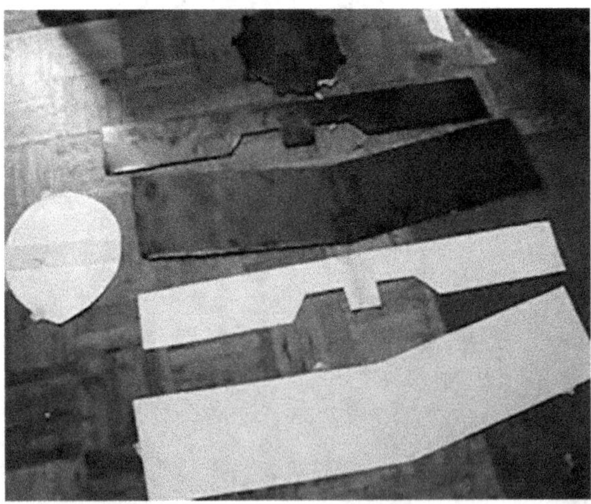

The major portion of this project comprises of a piece of rebar which was around 3 feet in measurement lengthwise. You will also need a side piece for around 1 foot to make the striking bar. The striking bar will be having an attached handle, to ring the bell.

In this project using rebar is the most cost friendly way of completing the project, but the sound produced by rebar is not that shrill. But it is enough if the house or hostel is not too big. However, you can make alterations as needed if you have some other material around.

First of all divide rebar into 3 equal portions, along its length. Next steps to heat up these portions in such a way that two points are bent together to form the triangle. Proceed with bending the bar. You will just give it a shape for a triangle but will not continue with closing the triangle.

 Next, you will go for making the upper portion of the head. Turn down a pine to get a cylindrical structure. Make some groves by turning it down. You can add up the color to make the handle brighter and attractive. Run the lathe with a low speed to make a mark with crayons and use a torch for heating up and melting the crayons.

An old saw is good to make a knife. The reason is that the meal used for the saw is usually of good quality and it can easily use to make a knife. There is no need to throw your old saw rather use if for making amazing knife.

To make the knife from an old saw, you will need these materials: pencil, chalk, old saw blade, cloth rags, hammer, scissor, acetone, coarse steel wool, cold chisel, vise, hardwood, handsaw, duct tape, light oil, power drill, sharpening system, cabinet scraper and sandpaper. Now learn that how to make a knife from an old saw blade.

Step 01: Sketch the design

First you need to sketch the design of your knife blade on some graph paper. Choose any design that you like. For the beginners, it's suggested that choose the simple designs to avoid troubles. Those people who usually work with blades can make any shape easily. Typically banana shape for the blades is very acceptable. But if you want some new design that is not easily available in the market, you can draw it by yourself and start working with it.

Step 02: Draw the design to metal

Now take your old saw and draw the design on it by using proper marks. There would be enough space available for you. From the single saw blade you can make many blades for the knives. Generally four to five pocketknives can easily be made by using the saw blade.

Step 03: Cut the outline

In this step you are required to cut the outline of your blade. Before cutting it, put a metal piece below it. Try to cut it properly so that you its shape doesn't change. Most people prefer to first cut a rectangular shape and later on they shape the blade. It's also another good way to cut the blade for your knife. If you want to get more knife blades out of one saw blade then it's not necessary to first cut the rectangular shape because in this way you will waste metal.

Step 04: Separate the blade

Now it's time to separate the blade from the metal piece. You can do it by simply putting the metal piece on the anvil and hammering it. Put the metal piece on the anvil in such a way that when you hit it with the hammer, the extra metal around the blade get separated.

Step 05: Shape the blade

The blade that you get in this way doesn't have best edges. So there is a need to file it properly so that you may get proper edges. Improper edges lead to several problems. First of all these are dangerous for your hands. You may get several injuries and cuts due to improper edges.

So shape the blade properly until its edges become soft and smooth. You can also notice the knives that are easily available in the market. They have very fine edges. Moreover if you want a knife with teeth, then this is the exception. But the teeth of your blade should also be properly and evenly designed. And the other sides must be smoothened.

Step 06: Make a handle

Now start the handle for your knife. It always remains good to use full tang. In this type of the knife, the blade is visible throughout the handle of the knife. For achieving this design, add scale of wood to each side of the handle and secure them later on with the rivets. If you don't want to make the wood handle by yourself, then there are many options available in the market. You can pick up any one of them.

Step 07: Set up rivets

Rivets look beautiful if you insert them properly. By using power drills make holes in the handle and tang. Equal and aligned holes make the work easier and look beautiful. Rivets are also available in variety of sizes and shapes to make your knife more enchanting.

Step 08: Shape as well as sand the handle
By using the file you can easily sand and shape the handle.

Step 09: Finish the handle for your knife
Proper finishing of your knife enables to last bit longer. For this purpose you can use oiled finishes because these are more durable and fancy. The thicker you choose oiled finishing, the more beautiful your knife looks. Apart from this, you are using an old saw blade to make a knife and there are several chances that it will get caught rust soon. So proper finishing gives the guarantee that it will last longer.

Step 10: Sharpen the blade
In the last step you are required to sharpen your blade properly. The sharp knives are good to work with. If the blade of your knife is not sharp then it's useless to keep it with yourself. There are several drills and files that are used to sharpen the blade.

In short, the above mentioned ten steps for making a good knife from an old saw blade are very easy. Follow these steps one after another and get a proper knife for use in home or some survival purpose.

CHAPTER 8

Your first knife

So, you've got some O1 tool steel (we call this piece of steel a *blank*), an assortment of tools and you're ready to go? Fantastic!

The shape that a knife can take is only limited by your imagination. That being said, this introduction to knives made through stock removal will take you through the creation of three particular knives. Each knife is designed to guide you through a few levels of difficulty and some templates are provided that you can copy by eye, trace, or scan and then print out at the size you need.

Now is the time to make mistakes, to be imperfect. I promise you, your first knife won't be the perfection you have in your mind. That will come in time and until then you've a lot of skills you need to sharpen.

For the readers that are currently recoiling in horror at these words: don't worry. I understand. I am quite the perfectionist myself but what I have learned over time is *when* to be a perfectionist. It's not always worth it. If I were to start any craft- as long as the financial cost of failure didn't wound me too much- I would try to make as many mistakes as early as possible. I would "polish a few turds" early on in order to get an idea of certain processes, but certainly not with the intent to make something perfect or worthy of that time spent.

You will have time to make your Masamune, your Excalibur, your Valerian dagger. For now, feel the liberation and make some knives with "personality"!

It's recommended that even if you want to skip straight ahead that you read through each project knife as each project contains explanations of valuable information. Finally, each knife will require heat treating which is detailed in the previous section. You might want to read about it in advance

A Throwing Knife

A throwing knife is a simple starting point for a few reasons. We don't need to make a handle for it, we can practice making bevels, and if you would like, practice establishing a cutting edge. As the cutting edge is not essential for a throwing knife's function you can experiment with less stress. Additionally, throwing knives are novel and tend to get most people quite excited.

1. Draw the Outline on your Blank

Cut out the template to the size you want, and draw its outline onto the blank with a marker pen. Keep the paper template as you can compare the shape of your knife to it in order to see what needs to change as you progress.

2. Cut out the Outline

This is called profiling. It's the act of taking your blank and giving it a fairly accurate knife shape.

You can use either a hacksaw or an angle grinder for this step. Remember which side of the pen outline you should stay on and consider that the closer you keep to the outline the less material you will have to remove with a file or belt sander.

There are a few ways you can cut out the outline. If you are using an angle grinder you might be able to directly cut along the outline. Otherwise, and especially if you're using a hacksaw, it's recommended that you put the blank in your table vise and cut perpendicularly to the edge of the blank until you reach the knife outline. Leave about a centimeter or less between each cut. This process of cutting segments along the knife's outline makes it easier to readjust your cut and to avoid accidentally cutting into the knife's profile. It also makes it easier to work around curves.

If you're using a hacksaw, this can take a while but keep at it. Get in the zone.

3. Neaten up the Profile

Using either a file or a belt sander with around around a 40 grit belt (it will work better if the belt has been "broken in" a little bit as this makes the grind less aggressive) neaten up the profile. Keep comparing it to the paper template- you can always remove steel… you can't put it back.

Filing the knife's profile requires you put it in your vise perpendicularly. The lower in your vise you keep the work piece the less it will bend and shake when you are applying force during filing. It is possible that you might accidentally bend the knife profile if it is held too high in the vise and it also makes the filing process a little less efficient and thus take longer.

Take a look at your outline and take note of where material needs to be removed. If your template or outline was applied with some care you simply need to adhere to it. If it was damaged or applied roughly you might need to bare that in mind in order to ensure symmetry and even curvature. This is why keeping the paper template is important as you can always lay the profile on top of the template to check your progress.

4. Mark the Cutting Edge and Centerline of the Blank

Mark a straight line from the tip of the blade to the tip of the handle on both sides. If you don't have a metal scribe you can sharpen a nail and that will work just fine. If you struggle to see the line you can use a pen to color the metal before scoring it, this help your line stand out.

A bevel is the angle on the knife that leads to the knife's cutting edge. We will be making 4 bevels overall, two on each side. The bevels should meet up on the centerline you just drew and also meet at the cutting edge. We should mark where the cutting edge should be too, that way we don't end up with an offset edge.

You can use a marking gauge if you have one and score where the cutting edge will be- directly in the center of the stock's thickness. If you don't have a marking gauge, never fear, there is trick you can do instead. Get a drill bit the same diameter as the thickness of your stock and clamp it to your bench. Drag the edge of the knife along the drill bit from where you want the cutting edge begins, to where it will end. You will end up with a decently centered line that you will use as a guide for the grind. Again, if you struggle to see the line, you can apply a colored marker before you score the steel to make the line stand out.

5. Grind the Bevel

There are a few different kinds of bevels you can put on a blade, each one with their merits and downsides.

Certain types of bevels come naturally to certain techniques- for example, using a rounded grinding surface such as a bench grinder, angle grinder or the rounded section of a belt sander, will result in what is known as a hollow or convex grind. This means that the cutting edge can be very sharp, but also fragile, as the edge will lack supporting material.

Another common bevel is a flat grind. This is achieved by using a file or belt sander to create the bevel from the spine (in this case the centerline) to the cut*ting edge. You will usually want to leave a narrow surface where the cutting edge will be in order to create a cutting edge* of a desirable angle. This secondary angle is- wouldn't you know it- referred to as the secondary or cutting bevel. Many kitched knifes are a good example of secondary bevels.

Though other grinds exist (other common ones include Scandinavian or convex grind) depending on what tools you are using I would recommend a hollow grind or flat grind for the throwing knife's bevel.

As the cutting edge doesn't matter as much as the point on a throwing knife I would recommend practicing a flat ground bevel. This is more likely to give you a more polished look if this is your first knife. Having said that, the next project relies on having a flat primary bevel and a flat secondary bevel. If you want to experiment with making a hollow ground bevel now might be the best time!

CHAPTER 9

Some Creative
Blacksmithing Projects

Decorative sword

Materials:

- Steel, 1 piece- 2 inches width, 36 inches length

- Steel, 1 piece- 1 1/4 inches width, 36 inches length

- Lump Charcoal (Hardwood)- 1 bag

- Wood, 1 piece - 2x2 inches

Instructions:

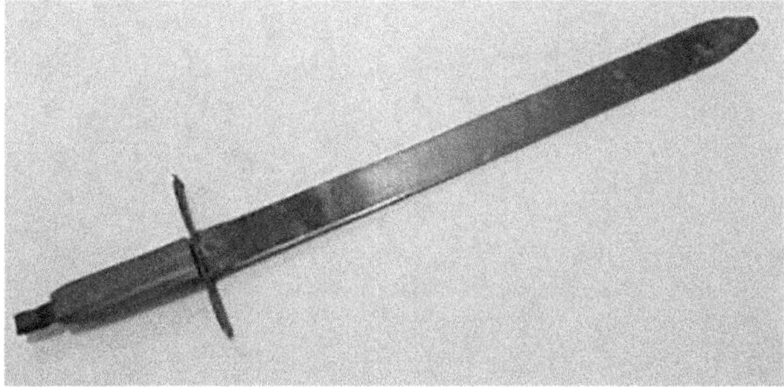

The steel piece used for making the sword will be hammered again and again so that it can make up a good position. The continuous hammering along the side of the metal piece is the most crucial step for making up the sword. It is usually regarded as squashing of the metal. The squashing results in making the edges of the metal thicker around the edges. The central portion of the metal piece will remain of the same thickness with which you started. Once squashing will be completed you will start with flattening of the metal piece in such a way that you will lay it out anvil and will flatten it out.

In order to attain the inner curve of the sword, you will need to continue with offset hammering. The side of the hammering that is affected. The side alongside the anvil will also be worked upon at the similar time. The rim of the anvil will be located where you want the placement of the drop coil. The blade part will be hanging across the anvil. The handle of the sword will lie over the anvil.

It will be done without finishing the surface of the blade. Hammering will enable you to get the exact shape of the sword. It will enable you to make a distinct drop.

Rondel

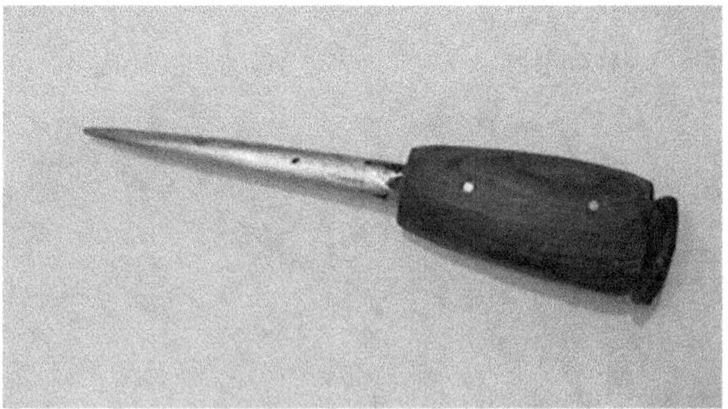

Materials:

- Anvil

- Hammer

- Metal strips

- Wooden handle

- Nails

Instructions:

The first step of this project relates to the picking of the Torch. You will need to get a propane torch which possesses a permanent button with ON instructions. This button is necessary for efficient working so that you may not need to permanently hold up the button for the supply of gas. It will not be possible while you will be using a forge. In the picture, you can see that the red button acts like a trigger, whereas the little metal button enables the locking of the trigger to enable permanent ON position.

The next step is to prepare the selected Can. Strip off any paint or plastic from the outer portion of the coffee can. Use a drill machine and make a hole at the side. The hole should be according to the nozzle of the torch so that it can fit into the hole easily.

Now treat the ceramic wool and cut it to a length which is suitable for covering the inside of the can. For covering the far end of the can a separate piece of ceramic wool will be needed. When the entire can is covered with the wool, the shape must be kept in a natural form without ant fasteners or adhesive. Now make a hole in the wool, right in front of the hole which you made for the nozzle.

Now make a base. You can continue with forging at this step as well but it is necessary to build a stand for the can so that the heated can may not distort or harm any of the table or chairs.

Based upon the particular angle at which the torch will be placed, you will adjust the base for the torch so that the hole at the can faces the nozzle without distortion.

The firebricks will provide a rough solid surface for keeping the metals on fire during the heat supply. Firebricks also aid in covering the gap at the front portion of the can so that content heat is provided. Now light up the torch and put the email object for forging. After successive heating sessions, use tongs to remove the metal. Place the heated metal over some hard surface. You can use a real anvil or concrete rock which will work out great. Now strike the metal several times for making any of the desired shapes.

Iron bell (hand forged)

Materials:

- Anvil

- Hammer

- Heating torch

- Metal strips

- Nails

Instructions:

The major portion of this project comprises of a piece of rebar which was around 3 feet in measurement lengthwise. You will also need a side piece for around 1 foot to make the striking bar. The striking bar will be having an attached handle, to ring the bell.

First of all divide rebar into 3 equal portions, along its length. Next steps to heat up these portions in such a way that two points are bent together to form the triangle. In order to give a clearer idea consider that of the rebar is 36 inches in length, you will be make two lines with chalk at two points. One will be at 12 inches and the next will be at a point of 24 inches. These points will make three quail portion for the bar. For heating, the bar follows the lines drawn. Proceed with bending the bar. You will just give it a shape for a triangle but will not continue with closing the triangle.

Candle holder

Materials:

- Anvil

- Hammer

- Metal strips

- Wooden handle

- Nails

- Heating torch

- Candle

Instructions:

You will start by forging the Jaw. Start by surrounding the end towards the near side across the anvil to under the half of the total original dimension. Wait for spreading the metal until it turns into the shape of the jaw of the tong. Now start with forging the Rivet Boss.

Continue with forging both the jaws in some symmetrical ways. You can easily weld on the reins. Distress and drag the ½-inch rod for the reins so that it gets prepared for welding. The easiest method for this is to bend around 3/8 inch of this end at 90 degrees and continue forging in such a way that it is out backward. Now place the assembled jaws over the anvil face.

Hit the rod solidly straight down in such a way that the rivet head is flattened. Keep rotating the tongs while forging the head. It will prevent any kind of bending over. When you will assemble the tongs, it will help you to organize the tong rack if space will be created in between the reins by finishing them in-between the rod. It will be according to the size of the tong rack which is at the back of the boss. In this way, you can alter the rivet tension so that it may open and shut with no trouble.

Decorative Door knocker

Materials:

- Anvil

- Hammer

- Metal strips

- Wooden handle

- Nails

Instructions:

The steel piece used for making the locker will be hammered again and again so that it can make up a good position. The continuous hammering along the side of the metal piece is the most crucial step for making up the locker. It is usually regarded as squashing of the metal. The squashing results in making the edges of the metal thicker around the edges. The central portion of the metal piece will remain of the same thickness with which you started. Once squashing will be completed you will start with flattening of the metal piece in such a way that you will lay it out anvil and will flatten it out.

In order to attain the inner curve of the locker, you will need to continue with offset hammering. The side of the hammering that is affected. The side alongside the anvil will also be worked upon at the similar time. So hammering comes to be the most important task for enabling perfect curves out of the metal piece. Make accurate use of the anvil surface and the horn.

The next step will be to dig the curve between the handle and the metal. For making that space you will continue with half face hammering. For this step, you will put the metal for locker half way over the anvil. The rim of the anvil will be located where you want the placement of the drop coil. The blade part will be hanging across the anvil. The handle of the locker will lie over the anvil.

CHAPTER 10

Proving Your Metal!

The phrase "proving your metal" entered the English language as a result of the blacksmith shop. While proving your metal in the modern workplace may mean showing what kind of person you are or "what you are made of". In the blacksmith shop it always meant one thing; hammering out quality metallic goods in the forge! In this chapter we are going to go over some of the best items and ways to create these items through blacksmithing.

The first item we are going to use to prove your metal as a blacksmith will also prove to be good at flipping pancakes and burgers because, yes, we are going to create a spatula! And now just any spatula! Our spatula will be made from a section of Coil spring to be exact. The Coil springs that we use could come from a wide variety of places. They could come from garage doors, garden wings, and many other household objects. Even the coils from your furniture should do fine for this exercise. These springs are handled best when they are cut into 5 inch sections on the cutoff wheel.

As soon as you have your 5 inch section cut from the spring place it in your forge and bring it up to a yellow kind of heat, this means that the heat that you use should not be too strong, but should be just about in between in range. During the heating process make sure that you keep turning this piece over and over just to make sure that the heat evenly encompasses the whole object in the fire.

After you have done this take out a pair of vicegrip pliers and lock them firmly on the half inch of the coil's end. Now with one quick pull the steel of the coil should easily unwind into one straight piece of metal.

If it's straight you know that your previous heating methods were correct, because if it doesn't come out straight and winds up as a wavy rod you will just have to straighten it later. But if the coil is straight you know that you have achieved what you set out to do; make a flat piece of metal out of a coil.

Now take this piece and saw off 12 inches in length and then heat it up to 2 and a half inches at the end. Flatten it to 1/16th of an inch with a regular blacksmith hammer. Use forceful, rapid blows to get your metal motivated, and try to maintain only one heating level during the entire process. Now grind the metal into the spatula shape that you want. Try to "clean grind" each side to make sure that it maintains an even one 16th of an inch in thickness.

And now reheat the blade until it turns to a dark kind of cherry red in hue. Now hold it up vertically and dip it in some oil. This helps you now if the blade dimensions are even. If the blade comes out of the oil without warping it means that it is of even dimensions. Otherwise the telltale signs of warped metal will let you know that it is in fact uneven. Once your blade is determined to be even continue shaping it until it is of the desired form for your spatula.

Our next item that you are going to produce is that of the common wrench. What shop couldn't use a wrench right? And these things couldn't be more easily made. They can be made in their complete form through the salvaged leafspring of a car. Just take a hot punch and use it to make a hole to the size that you need for the wrench. Now all you have to do is cut away any excess material and file the metal until it is at the appropriate size. After this place the your wrench back in the fire and temper it until it is purple in color. Cut open the ends with hammer and chisel head and the end result lends you a perfectly good wrench.

Another great steel tool that you can forge in your blacksmith shop is that of pliers. To make a pair of half an inch thick pliers, all you will need is a four inch wide heavy caliber truck spring leaf. Simply cut off a 12 inch section, heat it up and allow it to cool slowly. Now take the steel and scribe off on it the curved pattern of the pliers. While you are working out these curves make sure that you leave evenly spaced center punch marks for the holes and then drill these with a high speed drill.

Be sure to leave the holes spaced close enough to leave only paper thin divisions between them. After you have done this clamp the core section in your vise so that you can knock off all of the outer pieces. Now take the sharp ridges and file them off. The flattened ridges will be revealed again during grinding and filing. Now draw out the stock to form the two plier handles and then cut the piece in half and create two identical blanks. You can then forge the hinge sections, being sure to leave room for their full diameter.

After you have done this you can go ahead and further refine any flat surfaces you see on a motor driven side grinder. Each of your plier halves are now ready to come together, in order to put these two together, take the excess steel at the rim of the hinge and smooth it off with a file jig. You are going to have to file it back and forth and then flush with the bar jig, so that you can remove all excess steel from the rim of the hinge bearing surface. After this refinement, both halves should fit together.

Now you can place a hinge pin to hold the pieces together. With this pin attached place the assembly, flush on the anvil face. To cold rivet these pieces together you will need to use a 1 pound ball peen hammer, using both the ball and the fat of the hammer at different intervals.

Use the ball to hit the whole surface of the pin and then use the ball to force down the ridge texture that has been upraised by the ball. Simply repeat this process until the whole assembly is nice and tight, and once you are done, you have yourself a great new pair of pliers.

The next thing that we are going to fashion in our blacksmith shop is that of a metallic ring; just a round ring; a simple object that can serve many purposes; whether it is used on the farm or as a part for some sort of machinery. Knowing how to forge a circular ring is an essential part of smithing so lets get started. First off you are going to want to cut a piece of the stock to about 10 inches in length.

Take this piece and heat it until the metal is growing a cherry red, once you have obtained this heat square both ends of the piece. Now take the rod of metal you have and begin to bend about one third of it over the horn of your anvil and then bend the other end in the same way. Heat the center of the rod so that the ends begin to come together and soon you will have a metal ring looped all the way around the horn. Once the two ends bend and meet together allow it to dry and the end result is a solid steel ring.

For our fifth example of what we can do with a little blacksmith steel we are going to create a chain link. To do this, in a similar fashion as you did when you created the ring, take a cylindrical shaped piece of steel and place it over the horn of the anvil, now heat the center of the steel until the two ends begin to droop down and meet each other, now scarf the ends just like you did for the welded ring.

Now repeat this process to bend another link in the chain, before the metal is completely welded together take this link and attach it to the next, allow the metal to weld together in this linked chain and then repeat the process until you have added as many links as necessary. These chained links are great for a wide variety of projects and if you have enough material you can even make a chain link fence out of them. All of these projects are easy and at the end of the day very fulfilling, so go ahead, get busy, crank up the forge, put your hammer to the anvil and start proving your metal.

<h1 style="text-align:center">CHAPTER 11</h1>

<h1 style="text-align:center">Practice Techniques</h1>

When it comes to learning to heat and meld metal properly, there are a number of skills regarding, forging, welding and heat treatment that you will need to master in order to call yourself a blacksmith. A combination of these three categories of techniques is enough to create practically anything you can imagine. When practicing your new trade make sure to always take the proper precautions and wear gloves, eye protection and a flame retardant apron.

Forging

The first thing you will need to learn is how to forge properly as if it doesn't involve forging it isn't really blacksmithing. There are five primary forging techniques depending on what your end goal with the piece of metal you are manipulating will ultimately be.

Drawing: Drawing a piece of metal will make the piece of metal you are working with either wider or longer but it also makes it thinner. To perform this process, start by heating the part of the metal that you will be drawing until it is glowing bright read. Take the piece you are working on in a pair of tongs before setting it on your anvil and preparing to strike it with your hammer. When you do so, take note that the heated metal will move away from the point of impact and use this to your advantage.

You most likely won't reach your desired width or length before the metal you are working begins to cool. This is normal and it is important to avoid hitting the metal once it is no longer glowing as you risk breaking the piece you were working. You can decrease the number of times you need to reheat a piece by heating only the part of the piece you are working that you wish to draw.

If part of the metal spreads too far, turn the piece you are working on its side and hit it back the other way. This is also the basic method behind turning metal into shapes. Finally, you can use the peen side of your hammer to a series of divots in the metal in the direction you want the metal to move in before smoothing everything back out afterwards.

Bending: To bend a piece of metal you are working, start by heating only the portion of the metal that you wish to bend. Take one end of the piece of metal you are working and then rotate the other end in the direction you want the bend to take. This can be accomplished with two pairs of tongs or with what is known as a bending fork.

Bending can also be accomplished by placing the heated piece of metal onto your anvil with the portion you wish to bend sitting on the horn of the anvil before striking the metal so it bends around the anvil. Twisting the metal is done by simply turning the two ends of the metal in opposite directions. To unbend a piece of metal simply follow the same steps in reverse.

Upsetting: The goal of upsetting a piece of metal is to make the piece as a whole thicker by sacrifice either width or length. This process is more difficult to perform accurately than drawing and, as such, is used much less regularly. Begin by heating the portion of the piece of metal that you wish to upset before using tongs to firmly hold one end of the piece of metal against the anvil and hitting the opposite end with the hammer. This will then send the heated metal towards the end of the piece of metal that was pressed against the anvil. If your goal is to simply make one end of a steel rod or iron bar thicker than the other, you can also heat the metal item and then drop it against the anvil as well with the side you wish to be thicker pointed at the ground.

Punching: The goal of punching is to cut off part of the piece of metal you are working on, cause a section of it to become forked or simply put a hole into it. To do this, first heat the portion of the piece of metal that you wish to punch, remove it from heat and quickly place it on your anvil making sure to line up the part that is being punched with the hardie hole. You then take a slug, also called a punch, the size of your hardie hole, (or the peen of some hammers) line it up and strike the precise point with your hammer. Take care not to strike the hammer to the anvil directly as it can damage both objects and also possibly create shrapnel which can be dangerous.

Shrinking: Shrinking accomplishes much the same thing as upsetting but the methodology is different. It is useful when shaping things using what is known as a compound curve (for example, turning a flat metal sheet into saucer), which often leaves extra ripples in the metal. Shrinking compresses, the overall length of the metal, thus helping to flatten out these waves. To perform this technique, heat the metal to which you have applied the compound curve before placing one of the ripples on the anvil and striking it with the flat side of the hammer in a motion designed to compress the ripple as much as possible.

Welding

Welding using a forge is quite different from other forms of welding, and often more difficult, which is why many blacksmiths avoid it when possible. If you are interested in welding using just the tools you already have, there are four steps which are explained in detail below, briefly, they are cleaning the piece of metal you intend to weld, heating, joining and forging.

Cleaning: Prior to welding two pieces of metal together you will want to take a grinder, file or wire brush and ensure both pieces you plan on welding are as free of scale or rust as possible.

Heating: A propane forge is the best choice when it comes to welding as more traditional heating methods will result in a layer of smoke covering what you are welding and preventing it from taking properly. If you are using charcoal or coal, coat both pieces of metal with a product known as flux to keep everything as clean as possible, it is also useful with propane forges as it reduces oxidation.

To weld 2 pieces of metal together you will want to get them both as hot as possible, which means literally white hot. Don't go over this point however as all you will do is melt whatever it is you are trying to weld. Knowing the right temperature for your weld is simply a matter of practice as coming on too strong will result in a melted mess and anything beneath the required temperature will look like it welded properly while actually creating a subpar weld. If you are planning on putting strain on the weld you are making, make sure you test it beforehand.

Holding: Holding both of the pieces you are planning on welding together while also holding your hammer so the two pieces can become one is a difficult proposition only made easier with extensive practice. With that being said, there are a few tricks for making it easier.

- Loop a piece of metal back onto itself to create loops or eyes.

- Rivet the two separate pieces of metal together in a temporary fashion.

- Try a vise or clamp to hold the two pieces together temporarily.

- Get someone to help you (make sure you take the time to plan out who will do what and walk through the steps as the metal pieces will quickly drop from acceptable weld temperature to deceptively weak weld temperature.

Forging: When it comes to forging the two pieces of metal together, it is important always strike as quickly as possible while retaining a forceful and accurate down stroke. Before you begin, make sure you prepare yourself properly as molten metal, flux and slag will all fly from both pieces of metal you are attempting to weld. If the two pieces of metal cool before the weld is finished, it is important to reheat them as fast as possible without moving the weld point if at all possible. It is important to continue manipulating the work after the weld has been completed to ensure you are not putting undue stress on the weld point whenever possible.

Heat Treatment

The following techniques can be used to affect the natural hardness of the piece of metal being treated.

Hardening: To heat treat a piece of metal so that it becomes harder than it was before, heat the piece of metal until it becomes cherry red with the heat before picking it up with your tongs and dunking it in water so that the point you want to be the hardest enters the water first. Dunk the piece of metal into the water in as straight of an angle as possible to minimize the distortion in the way the hardening effect spreads.

If you find that your pieces of metal become brittle or shatter, consider dunking them in oil or salt water instead of regular water as these will help to let the metal cool more slowly. Alternately you can choose a metal with less carbon in it or temper the item before trying to harden it.

Annealing: Annealing is a process whereby metal is heated and then slowly cooled in an effort to decrease the number of stresses it contains internally, thereby toughening it significantly. To perform this technique, start by heating the piece of metal until it takes on a cherry red color before letting it slowly cool. The longer the cooling time, the stronger the result will be. If you find your items are cooling to quickly consider leaving them leaning against your forge or placing them in a pile of still warm ashes. If the piece of metal still seems to be cooling to slowly, consider leaving it in the forge and simply reducing the flames slowly instead.

Tempering: Tempering is a form of hardening that is most effective when you are looking to create something that has a sharp edge while also retaining its strength throughout. To successfully temper a tool, start by hardening it as much as possible before polishing the duller edge until it literally shines. Start heating the tool so that the sharp edge heats up first. As the heat moves, the shiny part of the tool will begin to change color, once it takes on a blue sheen dunk the tool in the water. Repeat this process until you achieve the desired results.

CHAPTER 12

How to Make Horseshoes

While in most situations you will be able to buy premade horseshoes and then simply fit them to the horse in question, if a situation arises where you need to make a shoe out of existing materials, it is best to be prepared.

Prepare the hooves

Prior to forging new horseshoes, you should first take the time remove the existing horseshoes and take care of the hooves themselves by first removing the existing nails by straightening them before removing them completely. Next you will want to manicure the hooves so they are smooth and even for the best shoe fit.

Size the hooves

Start by measuring the horse's hooves so you have an idea of the ultimate size the shoes should be. If you have to decide between shoes that are too big and those that are too small, always go with the larger shoes as they can be modified using the shrinking technique later on.

Make the shoes

For reference, most common horseshoes are constructed using A-36 steel bars which are then cut based on the width and length of the shoes required. Start by heating your piece of metal until it is red hot before forming it into the shape of a horseshoe using the processes discussed in chapter 4. Don't forget to punch out the space where the nails will ultimately go.

Depending on the resources at your disposal, new shoes can either be created (known as hot shoeing) or existing shoes can simply be bent into shape without heating them. While hot shoeing is considered much more time consuming, it also results in better fitting shoes 100 percent of the time. They will sit more evenly on the hoof and allow you to make more precise modifications. When hot shoeing, it is important to keep in mind the horse's feelings and not leave the hot shoe against the sensitive parts of the hoof for longer than necessary.

It is important to take all of the specifics of each hoof into detail, as oftentimes simple size and width are not enough. In addition, it is important to note that it is quite common for a horse to have hooves of several different sizes, make sure you measure each before committing to creating the shoe. The perfect shoe should reach the edge of the hoof without spreading out any further.

Shoe the horse

Once the shoes are crafted and cooled, nail on the new shoes making sure to avoid the inner parts of the hooves as they are extremely sensitive. Instead, place the nails so they go through at an outward angle. It is okay if the nail goes out the side of the hoof, as long as the center part of the hoof is intact. With the shoes attached take a large file (rasp) and file off the points of the nails. Take extreme care when performing this step as doing so incorrectly could hobble the horse for life.

CHAPTER 13

How to Make Blades

If you are interested in making any type of bladed tool or weapon, consider the following knife-making steps a rough blueprint of the steps you should take and substitute in the specifics for the blade of your choice.

Start by heating the metal: Steel is the best choice when making a bladed tool as it blends strength and durability like no other easily accessible metal. Place the metal into your forge and let it heat until the metal turns a golden yellow. This is very close to white hot so it is important to watch the temperature carefully to ensure you don't melt your material.

Flatten the metal: Remove the piece of metal from the forge using your tongs and place it on your anvil. Use firm precise strikes to make one edge of your piece of metal flat (the blade) and the other round (the spine). When forming the blade, don't forget to leave room for the part of the blade that fits into the handle (the tang). The tang should be at least two inches long if not longer depending on the length of the blade.

Make the blade: With an outline of your knife established, you can now more clearly define the blade by making a series of small taps up and down the length of the blade (repeating on both sides prevents distortion), this will narrow the edge of the piece of metal and will ultimately allow for the blade to hold a sharper edge.

Create bevels: Use your hammer on the flat portion of the blade to create the necessary bevels. While performing this step your blade will fold back on its spine somewhat, this is normal. When you notice this starting to happen, straighten the blade immediately. Letting this process proceed unchecked will allow inclusions to form, decreasing the amount of strength the blade will ultimately possess.

Let the blade anneal: Heat the blade and let it cool by setting it in a bucket of ashes twice before proceeding a third time and letting it cool in the forge overnight. This will make the bladed edge more malleable and easy to shape.

Shape the blade: Use a file to form the blade into your desired shape, taking this opportunity to smooth out any rough patches.

Harden the blade: Once you have finished shaping the blade place it back in the forge once more until it is red hot before dipping the side of the blade which will be used for cutting in oil to harden it even more. Take special care to dip only the cutting edge to create a blade that is durable yet flexible enough to provide the right amount malleability a good knife needs. Be sure to dip the blade as straight as possible, going in at the wrong angle will allow the metal to warp, forcing you to start all over again.

Finish the knife: Finally, all you need to do is temper the knife as desired, add a handle, sharpen it and enjoy. To sharpen it properly, start with a file before moving on to a whetstone.

CHAPTER 14

Beginner Tips and Tricks

Be patient

Many new blacksmiths are understandably anxious to begin hammering away at a piece of metal and with good reason, as it can be an extremely enjoyable process. Nevertheless, it is important to be patient and ensure your metal heats to the appropriate color before you pull it from your forge if you want to make the most of each hammer stroke. Pulling out pieces of metal when they are simply cherry red, rather than the dark orange you need them to be for proper forging, will do little for the piece of metal save make it look as though you beat on it with a hammer. What's more, pounding on an improperly heated piece of metal can cause it to break, forcing you to start over and wait even longer to get to the good part.

Watch your fire

Knowing that you only have a limited time with a piece before it cools can make it easy to focus on the forging process to the exclusion of all else as you strike while the iron is hot. While doing so, ensure you also take the time to keep tabs on you forge as without proper care your fire will dwindle or die and the time you waste getting it back to the proper temperature will be far greater than simply letting a piece of metal reheat.

Keep your forge clean

Many novice blacksmiths get so involved in their work that they don't take the time to properly clean their forge by removing the ashes from previous fires. In addition to creating sooty conditions that are less than optimal for proper forging, an excess of ashes can also raise injury concerns higher than normal. While it is normal for the fire in your forge to pop and spark from time to time, an excess of ashes will instead cause your fire to spark much more often and at a much greater degree. This is also why it is always a good idea to keep a shovel handy as coals that suddenly end up outside of the forge and perhaps on a pile of leaves need to be contained as quickly as possible to prevent serious fire damage from occurring.

Find your rhythm

Successful blacksmithing is all about proper timing and getting into the right pattern of striking and reheating can mean the difference between a job taking a single hour as opposed to 3. This is also why it is important to get into the habit of always keeping your tools in the same place near your anvil so that you don't have to waste precious time looking for them while the piece of metal you are working on proceeds to cool on your anvil. Get into this habit early as it is much easier to put 2 or 3 tools away into the same spot every time as opposed to 10 or 20.

CHAPTER 15

Sources of Steel and Testing

Steel is a very common material used in everyday life. We are surrounded by it, and it holds our modern world together. At its simplest, steel is an alloy of iron with a little carbon. The amount of carbon present determines how hard it can get through heat treating. Other elements, such as manganese, chromium, vanadium, nickel, and molybdenum, among others, can drastically change the properties of steel.

While there are many classification systems, one of the most universal is the SAE system, developed by SAE International. There is also the AISI (American Iron and Steel Institute) system that is very similar to the SAE. On top of that, different companies, steel mills, and manufacturers sometimes have special names or designations for the steel they produce. Other standards like the ASTM (ASTM International) classify steel based on its properties and not necessarily its components.

Simple steel, also called carbon steel, is simply iron alloyed with a little carbon. They may have some impurities that can affect some properties, but these steels generally react well to simple heating, quenching, and tempering. The amount of carbon in the steel determines how it will harden when quenched and other properties.

Steels with less than 1% added carbon are represented by a ten, and the amount of carbon is represented by the last sets of numbers, which are the percentage of carbon. So 1018 would be 0.18% carbon, and 1095 would by 0.95% carbon. Be aware that the numbers allow for some range of actual carbon and alloy content, sometimes as much as 0.05% in either direction.

If the steel has less than 0.3% carbon, it is considered low carbon steel and doesn't have enough carbon to really harden enough for making knives. It's considered mild or weldable steel, and it works well for making guards, pins, and other fittings. 1018 is an example of mild steel often used as a structural steel in construction.

0.3% to around 0.6% carbon is considered medium carbon steel. When hardened, the steel on the lower end is still quite soft. As the carbon content rises, the hardness increases. Steel over 1045 is often used for swords and machetes, and while it doesn't get very hard, it will work for knives.

High carbon steels have less carbon than cast iron, which starts at around 2.5% carbon. Even steel on the lower end can get quite hard and work well when hardened fully and tempered back. 1095 is one of the highest carbon simple steels, but another high alloy, tool, and stainless steels have more carbon. Steel high in carbon is capable of great hardness and strength and is commonly used for cutting tools, springs, and bearings.

Tool steels are alloy steels with one or many alloying elements. They are classified by their purpose or main characteristics with a letter. While some of these steels can be tricky to heat treat at home, some are more forgiving of beginning heat treaters. Some common knifemaking steels include O1, L6, W2, A2, M2, and D2.

O1, W2, and L6 can be treated in a similar way to simple carbon steel, with O1 being a good choice for the beginner because it is so forgiving. That said, tool steels perform their best when heat treated within certain parameters. The others require special heat treatment, and any drilling or rough shaping should be done before hardening. I suggest these steels be sent to a professional for heat treatment if you are starting out.

Stainless or stain-resistant steels usually have a high amount of chromium to resist corrosion and rust. There are lots of stainless steel, and some of the most corrosion-resistant work more like mild steel, making good guards, bolsters, pommels, caps, butt plates, and pins.

Many very popular and high-performance knife steels are stainless, and while some can be heat treated by eye with experience, most do best with carefully controlled temperatures. Like tool steels, I suggest beginning knife makers without the proper equipment send them out for heat treating.

There are many knife making supply companies online as well as specialty steel mills that sell steel for knife making. Low carbon steel can usually be found at most steelyards and hardware stores as weldable or mild steel. When I first started out making knives, I wasn't sure if it was something I wanted to invest a lot into, so I started out by repurposing other steel tools and unknown scrap steel.

Working With Heat Treated Steel

Another option for the beginning knife maker is working with steel that has already been heating treated. Cutting tools like files, blades, saws, machetes, and knives can be ground and shaped to make knives that need no or minor heat treatment. It's a great way to make your first knife and concentrate more on design than heat treatment.

Some tools and cutlery companies will provide the specifications of the steel they use, which takes some of the mystery out of reworking some knives. For example, the Ontario Knife Company uses 1095 in many of its machetes and kitchen knives.

Generally, most knife blades are already tempered and can be ground to shape to produce a good blade. This depends on the steel and type of treatment used, with most high carbon and performance steel knives being harder while more inexpensive knives, European-style kitchen knives, and most machetes tend to be on the softer side.

Saw blades are usually spring tempered, meaning they are very tough but too soft to hold a good edge without additional heat treating. That said, a spring tempered blade will still cut and hold a reasonable edge for a while. On the opposite side of the spectrum, files and rasps are usually left very hard and need to be tempered back to remove brittleness and make the finished blade tougher.

The most important thing when working steel that is already heat-treated or hardened is to keep it as cool as possible when grinding or sanding. Keep a bucket or container of water handy at all times and dip the blade into the water whenever it starts to feel warm. If possible, grind heat-treated blades without gloves or with very thin gloves so you can feel the heat. If the steel changes colors, you've lost the temper of that part of the blade, and it won't hold an edge for as long.

Junkyard Steel

If you have a piece of steel and don't know exactly what its composition is, you have a junkyard or mystery steel. Most tools, scrap parts, and building materials fall into this category. Sometimes it's possible to find out through testing or contacting the manufacturer what type of steel a tool or component is made of, but that only applies to that particular piece of steel.

For example, you may find a file and get confirmation from the manufacturer that it is made of W1 tool steel. Even though that file is known steel, other files may be made of other types of spring or tool steel. Even files made by the same company can vary from batch to batch. Some files are even made of mild steel or high-alloy steel that cannot be heat treated like simple steels.

It's better for the beginner to start out using the same type of known steel because getting a feel for heat treating is a lot faster when everything is consistent. There is much more of a learning curve when heat treating mystery steel, but it's possible to make very good blades with experience.

Some common sources of mystery steel are saw blades, old files, car and truck springs, chisels, and various woodworking tools. Many types of machines, mower, and harvesting blades also make good knives. Even softer steel found in many types of old tools and steel used in fabrication can make good chopping blades and machetes.

Since the alloy and carbon content of these and other sources of steel is a mystery, it's important to test any steel you find or are given to see if it will work for making knives. There are two basic tests that can help to determine the approximate carbon content and hardenability of unknown steel: the spark and quench test.

The spark test is quick and can be done to initially sort out different steels based on how much carbon they have and how hard they are. Once you get the hang of it, very little steel needs to be removed for this test. In the quench test, a sample piece of steel is heated to critical and quenched. The resulting brittleness and hardness of the steel let you know if the steel is hardened and to what degree.

While these tests will help gauge roughly if and how well a type of steel will work for the type of knife or tool you want to make, they are only rough approximations. Being able to figure out what the tests are telling you will also take time and practice, but the more you experiment and try, the better you'll get. There's something special about taking a piece of junk or an old worn down tool and giving it new life.

CHAPTER 16

Blacksmithing for Survival

This project uses two wide hooks and a store-bought wooden dowel.

1. First, you will make the points of the hook. Take an 8" round bar and anneal the end. On the face of the anvil, hammer the end to an even point. One blow should be made on the face of the anvil, and one blow is made by holding the hammer at an angle just off the edge of the face. When you become more experienced, this will be easier.

2. Anneal. Make a tiny scroll at the tip of the point.

3. Using the horn of the anvil, curve your piece in the opposite direction to create a circular "loop" for your dowel. Make the curve just a tad wider than the diameter of your dowel.

4. Anneal the other end of the bar. Flatten the end by hammering it on the face of the anvil. Hammer into a long fishtail shape. Punch two holes in this flat section about 1 – 2" apart. Your screws will go here and into the wall.

5. Repeat # 1 – 4 to make another loop for the dowel.

6. Measure the length of the dowel and place the loops to fit it. Slide your dowel through the loops and glue in place so the dowel won't roll.

7. Make notches in the dowel from which you will hang S-hooks that will hold your tools. Most tools have holes in them for that purpose.

Hammer

Hammers are extremely useful tools in every sense of the word. The ironic thing is that you will need a hammer while making the hammer. Making a basic hammer will involve a furnace and using extremely strong metal.

The first thing to be careful of is that many people will try and use scrap metals to make their metalwork. While it is entirely possible to use scrap metals for this purpose, you should be extremely wary of burning anything that isn't steel.

Steel will take the longest to melt, and other alloys will melt away, leaving you with the molten metal that will make your hammer.

Some of those alloys that burn away are toxic, and you do not want to be breathing any of them in. Be extremely careful and have quality ventilation systems in your forge to suck out any poisonous gas.

Once you have melted your metals that you will be using, a mold is needed to get the basic shape that you need. You need to let then it cool a little and trim the unwanted material.

Heat it a little more, so it is a little more malleable and keeps using your hammer to craft the desired shape. Remember that you need a big hole in the middle for the shaft of your hammer to go through. This should start to be formed after the first heat.

Once the shape is done, and it may take several attempts and several heats, put the shaft through the hole when the metal is almost cool but still a little flexible. Hammer it down, so it is firmly stuck in the hole, and you will have a reliable hammer. It might not compare to Thor's hammer, but you can certainly use it on future metalwork projects.

Axe

Hunters and lumberjacks across the land will tell you the value of a good axe. It is made in a very similar way to the hammer, except with the addition of a blade on end.

The important thing again is to watch what you are melting; some alloys are poisonous, and breathing them in can kill you or certainly cause some harm.

Heat your metal and pour it into the mold of the shape that you require. Then trip the edges and hammer your way to perfection.

Once the shape is correct, let the axe head cool for a while and sharpen the edge with a grinder. Sharpening is a whole other skill and can take years to perfect, but a grinder can get you most of the way.

Once fairly sharp, use a wet-stone to get it even sharper and hammer in your wooden shaft to make a super cool axe that can be used for a variety of (legal) purposes

Hunting knife

The hunting knife in the picture above looks both beautiful and lethal at the same time. It might take some perfecting to get the shape exactly right, but once you have mastered the art of forging, making products similar to the knife above will not be an issue.

Use good, solid steels in your work; it's always better to buy steel from a specialist place like a hardware store, even though it might cost a little bit more than using scrap. Heat the steel to the temperature on the manufacturing instructions of your forge and let any impurities burn away. Have a mold ready to get the basic sharp that you are looking for.

In a similar way to how we used a die for the horseshoe, dies are available and can be made specifically for knives. Once you have the shape you want, hammer away until it is perfect for you. Then trim away any excess metal and let it cool. Once cool, you can start to finish and polish the knife to give it an awesome color.

Add the wooden parts of the handle, depending on the design you have chosen, or wrap the string tightly as many do and polish again.

Sharpening is the last step when it comes to making a knife, and many would say it is the most important part. Chefs will tell you that sharpening a knife is an art form, and Japanese makers of Samurai swords will also tell you the same. Use a grinder to get the blade sharp, and then the rest can be done with a wet-stone. Have a chef show you the best way to sharpen a knife; they know all the tips and tricks of the business

Kitchen knife

Making a knife for the kitchen is no real difference from making a hunting knife, except for the fact that it might need to be a bit bigger and have a bit more weight behind it. With a knife for the kitchen, you are going for chopping action, while a knife for hunting will need to be used for a thrusting action.

Forge the metal, again using decent, high-quality steel and not your child's rusty bicycle frame. Use the die that you have to press the hot metal into the shape you require. Trim away the excess metal, finish, polish, sharpen into a blade on one side and starting chopping your vegetables.

CHAPTER 17

Heat-Treating Basics

Often called the heart and soul of knife making, heat treatment is an important aspect of the craft that consists of several different processes. One of the things that makes steel such an ideal material for making knives and other tools is how its properties can be altered by heating and cooling.

In this section, we'll go over some of the basic processes in heat treating and how they change the properties of steel. This is a stripped down version of heat treating steel geared for the first time knife maker. We'll also go over some options for the beginning knife maker who is unable to do their own heat treatment. We'll also go over how to start heat treating knives on your own.

The main heat treating processes in knife making are annealing or normalizing, hardening, and tempering. For simplicity, we're only talking about simple or low alloy steels in the medium to high carbon range because the different elements that are alloyed with iron to make a particular steel can greatly change how that steel reacts to heating and cooling.

In annealing and normalizing, steel is heated to a certain temperature and then allowed to cool slowly. The resulting steel is soft. Hardening is the process of heating steel to a certain point and then quenching (cooling it rapidly). This results in steel that is hard but also very brittle. Tempering takes steel that has been hardened and softens it, balancing hardness and toughness.

When steel is heated, its internal structure begins to change. When heating a clean piece of steel, it stays the same for a while and then starts to change colors. These colors are known as the tempering colors and are a way to estimate steel's temperature. After going through all of the colors, the steel darkens and then begins to glow.

The glow increases, starting out as a dull red and then to orange, yellow, and finally white. Steel begins to melt when white hot and still solid but very plastic when yellow to orange. When steel glows red, it is at an important transition point that determines many of its properties. Like the tempering colors, the color of the glowing hot steel is also a way to estimate temperature.

When steel is heated and begins to glow, it eventually reaches a point where it no longer sticks to a magnet. This nonmagnetic temperature marks a change within the steel. This is the beginning of the transformation range, which varies from steel to steel. During transformation, the internal crystal structure of steel begins to act more like a solution. The type of steel in this phase is called austenite.

When heated beyond the transformation temperature, steel becomes plastic and can be easily shaped and formed. This is usually called the forging temperature because the steel can be shaped with pressure. While we won't be doing any forging in this book, bent or crooked steel stock can be straightened at this temperature.

Now that we have a rough understanding of the different processes and how steel changes as it's heated, we'll dive a little deeper into each process starting with annealing and normalizing.

Annealing and Normalizing

A bucket full of perlite for cooling blades slowly

One of the first steps in heat treating is annealing or normalizing. Steel that has been hardened, worked, or deformed is internally stressed. It is the presence of these stresses that gives steel its hardness but is also what makes steel brittle. If you bend a steel paper clip back and forth, you'll notice that the steel gets harder to bend before finally snapping. It's the internal stress from being bent that causes the steel to harden and then break.

When annealing or normalizing, the steel is heated up until it is above the transformation temperature. At this point, the rigid crystal structure dissolves and becomes a solution of iron and carbon called austenite. When the steel is cooled slowly, the iron and carbon arrange into an evenly distributed crystalline structure. This structure is under very little stress and is called pearlite.

The difference between annealing and normalizing is time. When annealing, the steel is held at the transformation temperature longer and allowed to cool very slowly over the course of many hours.

When normalizing, the steel is brought up to the beginning of the transformation temperature and then allowed to air cool.

Both annealing and normalizing can be used to remove the stress from steel, but usually for different purposes. Annealing is usually done when steel that has been hardened through heat treating or work will be worked further. It helps to more or less reset the structure of the steel so that additional shaping or work won't cause cracks to form. It also makes it easier to work because the steel becomes soft.

Normalizing is usually done before hardening to remove the stress out of the steel and to help make the crystal or grain size more consistent. Heating a knife blade to the beginning of the transformation temperature and letting it cool in the air lets smaller crystals form. Smaller crystals end up giving steel more strength and an ability to resist breakage. We'll go over crystal or grain size more in the next two sections.

CHAPTER 18

Hardening

One of the most important aspects of heat treating a blade is hardening it properly. A properly hardened blade has a fine crystal structure and no cracks. This starts by normalizing the steel. By normalizing a couple (or a few) times, the grain or crystal size of the steel should be fine and the steel should be free of any major stress that could cause cracks or weak spots.

To harden the blade, it is heated up until it is non-magnetic and then brought up to the transformation temperature. It should be held there for a minute or so until the steel has converted into austenite. Then it needs to be cooled quickly. Oil, water, brine, or other liquids are often used to cool, or quench, the steel. If the steel is overheated before being quenched, the crystal size will increase and could make the steel more prone to breakage.

When the steel is cooled rapidly, the iron and carbon in solution cannot arrange into a fine pattern and the result is a highly-stressed crystalline formation called martensite. Martensite is very hard and brittle, but it can be tempered to change its structure and relieve stress to make it softer and tougher.

If the steel is not cooled fast enough or if the quenchant used is too mild, less martensite will be formed and will result in steel that is not completely hardened. Sometimes only the outside of the steel is hardened while the inside remains softer. Martensite is formed only during a brief temperature window, so it's important that the quenchant used matches the steel being hardened.

CHAPTER 19

What Quenchant to Use

In the last section, we went over how a knife is hardened by bringing it up past nonmagnetic and then quenching it. When steel begins to transform into austenite, it loses its ability to be attracted by magnets. This makes a magnet a great gauge to tell when a piece of steel has begun to transform. Once the steel has been heated a couple hundred degrees more, it is near the critical temperature and has fully transformed into austenite.

At this point, it's important that the steel does not get any hotter. This can be difficult as thinner edges and the tip of a knife are easily overheated. If the knife has been overheated, it is best to allow it to cool, normalize, and then start again. When steel is overheated, the size of the crystal structure known as the grain increases in size.

The piece on the left was overheated before quenching, producing a large and coarse grain structure.

Large grain makes steel less flexible and more prone to cracking and failing. Large grained steel is also more likely to crack during quenching. This change does not reverse, so letting an overheated area cool down to the critical temperature will not reverse the grain growth. At this stage, it's important to keep the color of the steel constant and even right up until the quench.

Ideally, the blade should be quenched as soon as it has fully transformed, but before grain growth can happen. When quenched, the steel goes through a second transformation into hard and brittle martensite. There is a narrow window of time and temperature that steel has to cool from near 1,500°F (~815°C) down to under 400°F (~204°C) in order for the austenite to become martensite.

How fast the quenching fluid or quenchant cools the steel depends on the steel and the fluid used. When the quench is too fast, stress builds up in the steel and can lead to cracks or internal fractures. A quench that is too slow will result in a blade that is only partially hardened. When the quench is just right, the blade is hardened fully without cracking.

Blade thickness also plays a big part when hardening. The thicker the blade, the longer it will take to fully reach the transformation temperatures inside. It will also take longer to cool the steel down quickly. This is why thinner blades are often more prone to warping and cracking than thicker ones.

There are many different quenchants designed for hardening steel that can be broken into three main categories. Some steel can be hardened in air or require the high temperatures of molten salt, but the main quenchants used for simple and low alloy carbon steel are oil, water, and brine.

Oil is the mildest of the three and cools a little slower than water and brine. Most medium and high carbon steels can be fully hardened in oil. Oil is very forgiving for the beginning heat treater because it's mild and lowers the chance of cracking or warping blades. Sometimes oil can be too mild for lower carbon or very high carbon steel, resulting in a blade with a hard edge or hard outer shell and soft inner core.

Many types of oil can be used for quenching steel, including many purpose-made quenching oils. I prefer to use vegetable oils with canola and peanut oils being my favorites. They work well, smell good, don't flare up as much as some oils, and are nontoxic. Motor oil and transmission fluid are also often used for quenching.

Keep in mind that oil can catch fire when hot steel is quenched. Always stay clear of the top of the quench tank and keep a fireproof cover like a steel plate or brick handy to cover the tank and snuff out any large flare-ups. It's a good idea to wear heavy leather gloves or use long tongs when quenching in oil.

Water is a more aggressive quench than oil that can work well for very high carbon steel, allowing it to harden deeper and eliminating the unhardened core that a slower quench can cause. If a piece of steel doesn't respond to an oil quench, water or brine may harden it.

The downside is that water is more likely to cause cracks and fractures in high carbon steel. Quenching a blade in water also creates steam that can keep the blade from cooling as quickly. It's a good idea to move the blade forward and backward as if slicing the water to help keep the steel in contact with water while quenching.

Brine is water with salt added and usually gives a faster quench than water because water vapor isn't as much of a problem. There are also various similar quenchants that use emulsifiers like detergents and soaps or surfactants to maximize the contact of water with the steel, resulting in a very aggressive quench that can harden medium carbon steel, but can also shatter high carbon steel.

When starting out, use oil. It's a very forgiving quench and while it can sometimes be too mild and keep a blade from fully hardening, it's also less likely to cause cracks in the steel. The shallow hardening of oil on some steel types can also be an added benefit when making larger knives that will be subjected to a lot of heavy chopping as the softer core can help keep the blade from breaking.

A final note about quenching is a full versus a differential quench. In a full quench, the steel is brought up to critical and then cooled all at once. This results in a blade that should be uniform in hardness. With a differential quench, the blade is brought up to critical and only part is allowed to cool quickly. This partial quench results in a blade that is only hard where it was quenched.

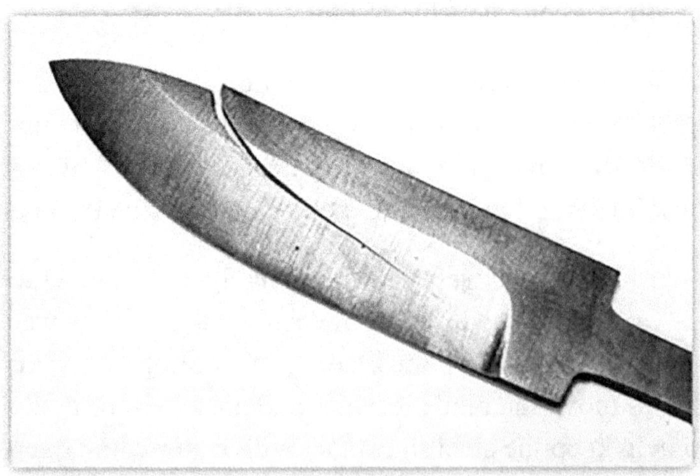

This can be done in a few different ways, the simplest being the edge quench. With an edge quench, only the edge of the knife is cooled in the quenching medium and the rest of the knife cools slowly in air. While this produces a blade with a soft back that can resist breaking, the strain of the edge quench can cause cracks or fractures. Edge quenching should only be done with a quenchant that is mild for the steel used.

For example, edge-quenching a high carbon steel blade in water can cause the blade to crack along the quench line while a full-quench would work well. This is because fully-quenching the knife puts everything under the same stress while with edge-quenching, the stresses are uneven and focused where hard and softer steel meet.

Another way to differentially quench is to coat part of the blade in clay or another insulator. When the blade is quenched, the uncoated areas cool faster while the coated areas cool slower. This method allows for a greater degree of control over the areas hardened. Clay hardening can result in a very striking visible line between hard and soft steel which can be seen on Japanese swords and has become very popular for all sorts of modern blades. This is often referred to as the hamon.

Tempering

After steel has been hardened, its structure is very stressed and brittle. Some of this stress can be relieved through tempering, which can have a similar effect as annealing. To temper steel, it is brought up to a temperature much lower than when annealing and then allowed to cool quickly.

As steel is heated, a thin layer of oxide (like rust) forms on the surface and protects the steel. After a certain point, the oxide starts changing color and will shift through a rainbow before turning gray. The color of the oxide layer can be used to determine the approximate temperature of the steel and the hardness of the steel.

Just like hardening, certain steels react differently than others when tempering. Judging the proper temper by color is a skill, which is why most large scale or precision tempering is done by measuring temperature directly, not color. When tempering in an oxygen-free environment, the colored oxides don't form at all.

As martensite is heated, it starts to degrade as the crystal structures begin to break up. This makes the steel softer and less brittle as it is no longer under the same amount of stress. As a very hard steel is tempered it will not only become softer but will also gain a springy quality. A piece of steel that started out very hard and is tempered back is usually much more resistant to taking a bend or breaking than a similar piece of steel that was incompletely hardened.

For the maker just starting out, tempering can be tricky to master. In the build-alongs, we'll go over three simple ways to temper a blade using a torch, oven, and hot coals. While not very precise, reading tempering colors is a good skill to develop. With practice, it's not difficult to bring a blade down to particular hardness with simple methods.

Along with an even temper, a blade can also be selectively tempered to make certain parts softer than others. This is commonly done by tempering the spine of a knife back, resulting in a hard edge, soft or springy back, and a springy center. The result is similar to incomplete or differential hardening but tends to be easier to control when starting out.

Since it takes longer for the steel inside of a blade to heat up than the outside, heating too fast will soften just the outside while leaving the inside untempered. This is why it's a good idea to take your time with tempering, getting the steel up to temperature in about an hour or so. It also helps to temper more than once to the desired color to help ensure the steel is evenly tempered.

When using an oven, use an in-oven thermometer to make sure the temperature is correct. As long as the temperature stays even and does not rise over the wanted temperature, your results will be reliable. Another way to help with more even heat is to place the blade to be tempered in the middle of a pan filled with sand. The sand helps keep the heat even as there may be hot spots in the oven.

The tempering colors run from a very light straw through gold, brown, purple, and then into blue. After blue, it lightens up and takes on a dull gray color. The exact temperature of these colors depends on the particular alloy, but the temperature of light straw is about 350°F while the temperature of blue is around 550°F.

You can find the tempering colors in full color on the back cover of this book. I suggest taking a look at other tempering charts as well to get a feel for tempering colors and temperatures. There are many metallurgy manuals available and most steel suppliers will also have heat treating charts for their steel.

In practice, the softer a knife is tempered, the tougher it is. The drawback is that as hardness goes down, edge holding ability tends to go down as well. A light yellow temper is good for most smaller knives or those that need a hard edge and will mostly be used for fine cutting tasks. Larger knives or heavy use knives do better with a straw to dark straw temper, making them soft and resilient enough to resist impact or chipping but still hold a good edge.

I usually do a brown to magenta temper on swords, machetes, and heavy chopping tools like axes that need to withstand constant impact and abuse, with fine edge holding less of a concern. A full blue temper is very springy and good when making parts or blades that need to flex and return without taking a set or breaking.

Sending It Out

Once I had started making knives, I really wanted to work with stainless steel and feel confident in selling my work. I didn't have the skill or the equipment to confidently heat treat those blades myself, so I did what many custom knife makers do: send them to a professional for heat treating.

There are many types of steel that have qualities ideal for knife making due to different elements mixed into the steel. These are high alloy steels and include stainless steels. One of the problems with these steels is that they are often difficult to heat treat without specialty equipment or lots of experience with heat treating by eye.

Even O1 tool steel, considered one of the more forgiving steels for the beginner, performs much better when precisely heat treated. Most high alloy and stainless steels cannot be hardened in a quick quench and need to be soaked at certain temperatures for longer periods in order to harden properly.

There are many companies that will do heat treating for you. Some are larger firms, some are smaller companies while others are just individuals. Some knife makers who have heat treating ovens or who are confident in their personal skills may also offer to heat treat blades.

Having your knives heat treated by someone else may be a little pricey, but if the person or company is reputable and does a good job, it's well worth it. You'll have the confidence knowing that your blades are the exact hardness you ask for. Some larger companies can also do different services including cold and cryogenic tempering to improve strength and wear resistance on certain steels, something that is usually cost prohibitive for the average knife maker.

It's a great option if you really want to hit the ground running in terms of selling knives. You'll also get an idea of what a properly heat treated blade should perform like if and when you decide to do it on your own. If done right, blades will come back to you looking just like you sent them, saving you time on refinishing before attaching handles.

There are some things to keep in mind, however. Since each type of steel works best with its own heat treating process, heat treaters will generally only accept knives made of known steels. Some will also only take on orders with a minimum of knives. This can work out as a benefit as most will also offer discounts on bulk orders as well.

Another option when getting started is to work with kit knives. Kit knives run from pre-heat treated blades that require finishing to full kits that only need some assembly. They are a great way to practice finishing handles and getting a feel for building knives. Many knife companies and custom makers also offer knives without handles at a reduced price, which is a great way to build a small collection of other people's work at a lower cost.

Finally, you can also do minor grinding and shaping work to finished knives as practice. There are many knife makers who started out re-grinding and putting new handles on butcher knives and old blades while retaining the original heat treatment. Large knives and blades like machetes can also be cut down and used like already heat treated knife stock. We'll go over this a little more in the next section on selecting steel and in our first knife build in chapter 3.

Sources of Steel and Testing

Steel is a very common material used in everyday life. We are surrounded by it and it holds our modern world together. At its simplest, steel is an alloy of iron with a little carbon. The amount of carbon present determines how hard it can get through heat treating. Other elements such as manganese, chromium, vanadium, nickel, and molybdenum among others can drastically change the properties of steel.

While there are many classification systems, one of the most universal is the SAE system, developed by SAE International. There is also the AISI (American Iron and Steel Institute) system that is very similar to the SAE. On top of that, different companies, steel mills, and manufacturers sometimes have special names or designations for the steel they produce. Other standards like the ASTM (ASTM International) classify steel based on its properties and not necessarily its components.

In the SAE system, a steel's alloy is represented by letters numbers. With alloy steel, the first number represents the main alloying element while the other numbers represent amounts or if the steel has multiple alloying elements. Steels that work best with the heat treating methods in this book are simple steels, represented by 1 plus three numbers (1XXX).

Simple steel, also called carbon steel, is simply iron alloyed with a little carbon. They may have some impurities that can affect some properties, but these steels generally react well to simple heating, quenching, and tempering. The amount of carbon in the steel determines how it will harden when quenched and other properties.

Steels with less than 1% added carbon are represented by a 10 and the amount of carbon is represented by the last sets of numbers which are the percentage of carbon. So 1018 would be 0.18% carbon and 1095 would by 0.95% carbon. Be aware that the numbers allow for some range of actual carbon and alloy content, sometimes as much as 0.05% in either direction.

If steel has less than 0.3% carbon it is considered low carbon steel and doesn't have enough carbon to really harden enough for making knives. It's considered mild or weldable steel and it works well for making guards, pins, and other fittings. 1018 is an example of mild steel often used as structural steel in construction.

0.3% to around 0.6% carbon is considered medium carbon steel. When hardened, the steel on the lower end is still quite soft. As the carbon content rises, the hardness increases. Steel over 1045 is often used for swords and machetes and while it doesn't get very hard it will work for knives.

High carbon steels have less carbon than cast iron, which starts at around 2.5% carbon. Even steel on the lower end can get quite hard and work well when hardened fully and tempered back. 1095 is one of the highest carbon simple steels, but other high alloy, tool, and stainless steels have more carbon. Steel high in carbon is capable of great hardness and strength and is commonly used for cutting tools, springs, and bearings.

Tool steels are alloy steels with one or many alloying elements. They are classified by their purpose or main characteristics with a letter. While some of these steels can be tricky to heat treat at home, some are more forgiving of beginning heat treaters. Some common knifemaking steels include O1, L6, W2, A2, M2, and D2.

O1, W2, and L6 can be treated in a similar way to simple carbon steel, with O1 being a good choice for the beginner because it is so forgiving. That said, tool steels perform their best when heat treated within certain parameters. The others require special heat treatment and any drilling or rough shaping should be done before hardening. I suggest these steels be sent to a professional for heat treatment if you are starting out.

Stainless or stain resistant steels usually have a high amount of chromium to resist corrosion and rust. There are lots of stainless steels and some of the most corrosion resistant work more like mild steel, making good guards, bolsters, pommels, caps, butt plates, and pins.

Many very popular and high-performance knife steels are stainless and while some can be heat treated by eye with experience, most do best with carefully controlled temperatures. Like tool steels, I suggest beginning knife makers without the proper equipment send them out for heat treating.

There are many knife making supply companies online as well as specialty steel mills that sell steel for knife making. Low carbon steel can usually be found at most steel yards and hardware stores as weldable or mild steel. When I first started out making knives, I wasn't sure if it was something I wanted to invest a lot into, so I started out by repurposing other steel tools and unknown scrap steel.

CHAPTER 20

Working With Heat Treated Steel

Another option for the beginning knife maker is working with steel that has already been heat treated. Cutting tools like files, blades, saws, machetes, and knives can be ground and shaped to make knives that need no or minor heat treatment. It's a great way to make your first knife and concentrate more on design than heat treatment.

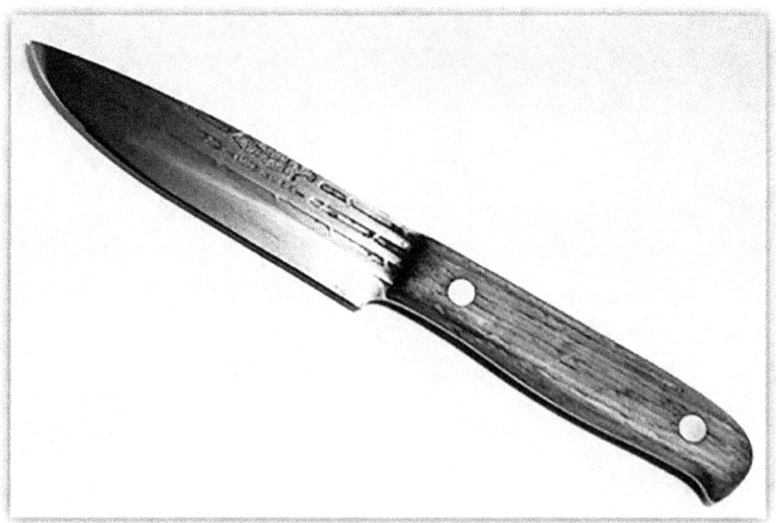

This shortened and re-ground butcher knife makes for a good all-around utility knife.

Some tool and cutlery companies will provide the specifications of the steel they use, which takes some of the mystery out of reworking some knives. For example, the Ontario Knife Company uses 1095 in many of their machetes and kitchen knives.

Generally, most knife blades are already tempered and can be ground to shape to produce a good blade. This depends on the steel and type of treatment used, with most high carbon and performance steel knives being harder while more inexpensive knives, European-style kitchen knives, and most machetes tend to be on the softer side.

Saw blades are usually spring tempered, meaning they are very tough but too soft to hold a good edge without additional heat treating. That said, a spring tempered blade will still cut and hold a reasonable edge for a while. On the opposite side of the spectrum, files and rasps are usually left very hard and need to be tempered back to remove brittleness and make the finished blade tougher.

The most important thing when working steel that is already heat treated or hardened is to keep it as cool as possible when grinding or sanding. Keep a bucket or container of water handy at all times and dip the blade into the water whenever it starts to feel warm. If possible, grind heat treated blades without gloves or with very thin gloves so you can feel the heat. If the steel changes colors, you've lost the temper of that part of the blade and it won't hold an edge for as long.

Junkyard Steel

If you have a piece of steel and don't know exactly what its composition is, you have a junkyard or mystery steel. Most tools, scrap parts, and building materials fall into this category. Sometimes it's possible to find out through testing or contacting the manufacturer what type of steel a tool or component is made of, but that only applies to that particular piece of steel.

For example, you may find a file and get confirmation from the manufacturer that it is made of W1 tool steel. Even though that file is a known steel, other files may be made of other types of spring or tool steel. Even files made by the same company can vary from batch to batch. Some files are even made of mild steel or high-alloy steel that cannot be heat treated like simple steels.

It's better for the beginner to start out using the same type of known steel because getting a feel for heat treating is a lot faster when everything is consistent. There is much more of a learning curve when heat treating mystery steel, but it's possible to make very good blades with experience.

Some common sources of mystery steel are saw blades, old files, car and truck springs, chisels, and various woodworking tools. Many types of machine, mower and harvesting blades also make good knives. Even softer steel found in many types of old tools and steel used in fabrication can make good chopping blades and machetes.

Since the alloy and carbon content of these and other sources of steel are a mystery, it's important to test any steel you find or are given to see if it will work for making knives. There are two basic tests that can help to determine the approximate carbon content and hardenability of unknown steel: the spark and quench test.

The spark test is quick and can be done to initially sort out different steels based on how much carbon they have and how hard they are. Once you get a hang of it, very little steel needs to be removed for this test. In the quench test, a sample piece of steel is heated to critical and quenched. The resulting brittleness and hardness of the steel let you know if the steel is hardenable and to what degree.

While these tests will help gauge roughly if and how well a type of steel will work for the type of knife or tool you want to make, they are only rough approximations. Being able to figure out what the tests are telling you will also take time and practice, but the more you experiment and try the better you'll get. There's something special about taking a piece of junk or an old worn down tool and giving it new life.

Spark Test

When a piece of steel is ground with a powered grinder it will give off sparks. Depending on the grit and type of grinder used, it can vary from a full shower to a few individual sparks. By watching both the amount and shape of individual sparks of different steel you can get an idea of the steel's carbon content and hardness.

This test requires a power grinder or belt sander in order to get a nice display of sparks. Keep in mind that sparks are very hot and can start fires. Always be aware of where sparks are going and make sure to clean off any wood dust from the area or grinder before grinding steel. Ideally, you should have separate grinders for steel and everything else.

Here's the file on a coarse grinding disk. You can see many sparks with lots of little bursts per spark. These look like sparks that give off their own sparks.

The mild steel also gives off a shower of sparks, but these look longer and only a few have any bursts at all.

With a 150 grit belt, you can clearly see the complex bursts of the sparks from the file. There are lots of sparks because the file is hard.

The mild steel has very simple sparks with very few bursts. There are also very few visible sparks because the mild steel is soft.

This knife is made of 1095 that has been tempered. You can see the edge produces many complex sparks showing it is high carbon and hard.

The back of the knife was torch softened and gives off very few sparks. You can still see that the sparks are more complex than mild steel.

Before testing unknown steel, get an old file and a piece of mild steel. These will be a baseline so you can get a feel for what high and low carbon steel looks like. If you have access to known steels, you can use those as well to compare against mystery steel.

Start with a coarse wheel, disk, or belt on your grinder of choice. Turn it on and grind the file. There should be a large shower of bright sparks that have multiple bursts and lots of little trails per spark. Grind the mild steel. If the sparks look similar to the file and you can't really tell them apart, switch to a finer grit. The mild steel should have finer sparks with only a little burst at the end. If the file still looks the same as the mild steel, try another file, as it might be made of case hardened mild steel.

I find that with 120-150 grit, low carbon steels show few sparks while high carbon steel shows lots of complex sparks that are easily visible. Once you can pick out the big differences between high carbon and low carbon steel, it's time to try out a piece of mystery steel.

Pay attention to how the sparks look instead of the number of sparks. More sparks mean the steel is harder while fewer sparks mean the steel is softer. Low, medium, and high carbon steels can have different amounts of sparks depending on their hardness, but the way the sparks react are fairly constant.

Low carbon steel will give off a shower of simple sparks that look a lot like straight lines of light with a few little bursts mixed in. Since low carbon steels don't harden, they usually show fewer sparks when using a higher grit wheel or belt.

Don't be surprised to find hard steel with simple sparks because low carbon steel can be work hardened like non-ferrous metals. Also keep in mind that some tools or blades are made of low carbon steel that has been case hardened, which is a process that allows carbon to soak into the steel, giving it a thin skin of hardenable steel over the soft core.

Steel in-between the carbon content of the file and mild steel can be tricky to pinpoint with this test. It helps to test a piece of medium carbon steel to get a better idea of what it looks like. Most hardenable steel will look similar to the file and while there may be slightly fewer bursts, they should still have multiple branches. If you are unsure, try the quench test. If it hardens, keep it as an example of a hardenable steel for future tests.

Sparks from high carbon steel will look like the file. Most files have a lot of carbon, usually being made of 1095 or other high carbon tool steel. If the steel being tested looks similar to the file or has more complex sparks, it's probably a high carbon steel of some sort.

Steel with a certain amount of carbon will show the same types of sparks regardless of hardness, it's just the amount of sparks that changes. Watching sparks is a good way to gauge relative hardness. The more sparks you see, the harder the steel. This is a good way to test the edge of a knife after heat treating because sometimes the very outside of the steel has lost carbon and is soft and a little grinding can expose the hardened steel edge.

Quench Test

If a piece of steel seems to have a good amount of carbon in the spark test, the next step is to see if it can be hardened and by how much. This is important because some high alloy steels that are high carbon cannot be heat treated like simple carbon steel. It's also a way to further refine reading sparks.

To start, take a piece of mystery steel, heat it up to critical, and then quench it in oil. Use a file to test the hardness of the surface of the steel by seeing if the file scratches it. If the file just slides and doesn't scratch the steel, the next test is to hit the hardened portion with a hammer. If the steel shatters, then it's likely that the blade has hardened deeply. This steel should make a good knife.

If the steel does not shatter but the edges break or cracks form, it means the outside of the steel hardened but the inside is still soft. Heat a new portion of the steel and quench it in water instead. The file should still slide and if a hammer shatters it, then it should have enough carbon to make a good knife, though it may only harden at the edges if using oil.

Steel that is harder than a file but doesn't crack or break under the hammer can still be made into a knife. If a file cuts into the steel, it means the file is harder. Hardness in knife steel is often measured on the Rockwell scale, which bases hardness on how deeply a piece of steel is indented under a set pressure. Most files are around 60-65HRC on the Rockwell scale.

Knives usually fall around 55-62HRC or so, with knives higher-up holding a better edge and those on the lower end being tougher. This is true of simple steel that is hardened and then tempered back. If a piece of steel is harder than a file, that means it can be tempered back. Medium carbon steel can often be hardened enough to hold a good edge without tempering, ending up somewhere in-between.

Keep in mind that these test won't tell you exactly what a steel is and it takes practice and experience to really learn how to read steel. These test will help figure out how to treat what you have if you only have access to unknown steel, but know that there is a much steeper learning curve. It's always good to start out learning with known steel or at least the same type of steel.

CHAPTER 21

Safety and Precautions

Making knives can be extremely rewarding and fun, but there are risks. Knives themselves can cause damage and harm if misused or handled improperly. Working with tools, especially with power tools, can be dangerous. While there are risks, using the right safety equipment and understanding the risks can help you avoid risky situations. And if anything does happen, keeping calm will help you get through it.

Safety Equipment

It's important to always wear the right clothing and proper safety equipment when making anything, especially knives. Wearing long pants can help protect you from sparks and flying debris. A good leather apron also adds protection. Avoid wearing anything loose fitting that could get caught in a power tool, including loose long sleeves.

Remove any watches or jewelry (even wedding bands) before operating power tools or dealing with fire. Keep long hair secured and it's also a good idea to have your hair covered when operating a forge. Covered shoes are a must and I highly recommend steel-toe shoes or boots.

When doing any sanding, cutting, or grinding, good lung protection is very important. Any dust is bad for your lungs, especially the silica grit found in many grinding wheels and sandpaper. Exposure over time can cause irreversible damage, so make sure to protect your lungs. Find a good respirator that is rated for the type of material you're grinding or sanding and make sure to keep it clean and replace filters when needed.

A good pair of safety glasses or goggles will help protect your eyes while doing light work. For heavy grinding, buffing, drilling, and cutting, a full face-shield over the glasses will help protect both your eyes and face from flying debris. A face shield can also help your respirator from getting clogged too quickly when sanding. Always remember to wear eye protection, it could save your eyes and your vision.

Gloves come in many different styles. I personally use a pair of heavy leather gloves when doing a lot of angle grinder work as they help cut down on vibrations. A good pair of gloves can protect your hands from minor cuts and abrasion when filing and cutting as well as when handling sharp and jagged material. I don't use gloves when grinding with a bench or belt grinder so that I can feel if the metal is getting hot. One downside to gloves is that they can get caught by some power tools and pull your hand into the machine.

CHAPTER 22

Working With Power Tools

Power tools are great time-savers, allowing work to be done much faster and in many cases more efficiently. One of the things with power tools is that they usually go fast and It's important to always be aware before things go wrong. Make sure that everything is in order and the tool is clear before turning it on.

Safety equipment is very important when using power tools. Powered grinding and sanding produces very fine dust that usually gets kicked into the air more readily than with hand tools. When grinding metal, power tools produce sparks that can start fires, so make sure the work area is clear of any flammables.

When a tool is running, pay attention to what you are doing. Never take your eyes off the machine and if you have to look away or do something else, stop what you are doing and turn the machine off first. I have seen people lose bits of fingers because someone called their name and they looked over while a machine was still running. Things can happen very quickly if you aren't paying attention.

Keep distractions to a minimum and do not operate any power tools or work with fire while intoxicated. Only work with power tools if you are calm and have a cool head. I know that for me, making things is a great way to calm down and relax, but it's easy to get distracted if you are upset or not thinking straight.

Keep calm. If anything does go wrong, don't panic. If you are hurt, try to turn off the machine or cut power and step away. Leaving a tool running or an angle grinder skittering across the floor could cause more damage. Make sure you have a way of getting help quickly just in case.

It's also good to keep a clean shop and have some sort of order to it. Not only is it safer this way, but it's a lot easier to work when you know where everything is when you need it.

Working With Fire

While it's possible to make knives without any heat or power tools, chances are you'll be working with fire or showers of sparks. Fire can spread quickly, so it's always good to have a plan for preventing any uncontrolled fires and dealing with it if things go awry.

Be aware of your surroundings and make sure than any sparks you make won't end up in anything flammable. Wood dust and shavings, dry grass, flammable gas or solvents, oil, and cloth (especially oil-soaked cloth) should be kept away from possible sparks.

Any fires or burning gas should be done outdoors or indoors with extremely good ventilation. Carbon monoxide poisoning is serious as well as inhaling smoke. If you do any work with a torch or forge indoors, always make sure to check for gas leaks either in tanks or in gas lines if your house or apartment has gas. Also be aware of sparks when working on a wood floor or deck, especially if there are gaps where a fire could start.

When quenching knives in oil, it's common for the oil to flare up. Make sure to keep your face and hands away from the top of the quench tank to avoid burning yourself. If a flare up does happen and doesn't put itself out in a few seconds, place a non-flammable lid over the tank to cut off oxygen. Never try to put out an oil fire with water.

Keep a fire extinguisher handy and make sure you're comfortable using it. Stay calm if a fire does happen because it can sometimes be disorientating especially if you can't find the source right away. If the fire gets out of control, evacuate the area and get to safety.

Tools and Sharpening

In this chapter, we'll go over some basic knifemaking tools for the beginner as well as other helpful tools and the three main ways to heat blades for heat treating. We'll also go over how to sharpen knives at the end of the chapter. The tools that we'll be using in this book are simple and inexpensive, great for starting out in this hobby without spending a lot of money on tools.

First we'll look at power tools and then go into some helpful hand tools. While knives can be made with hand tools alone, power tools can make the work go by much faster, especially when working with tough materials and hardened steel. The two main tools used are the angle grinder and power drill because they are able to do the work of several different machines but if you plan on using other tools, the same methods can be applied.

Power Tools

Angle Grinder

If I could only have one power tool for making knives, it would be the angle grinder. It is incredibly versatile and can be used for grinding, cutting, and cleaning up metal, as well as shaping, sanding, and finishing wood and other materials. In a lot of ways, the angle grinder in an all-in-one tool for the beginner knife maker in a budget.

There are different sizes of angle grinder, with 4-1/2 inch diameter grinders being one of the more common sizes. 4 and 4-1/2 inch grinders are great for smaller work and can be found very inexpensively. Even machines with smaller motors are enough for making knives. The larger sizes are great for cutting stock or for more aggressive grinding.

When using grinding and cutting disks, angle grinders are great for cutting and shaping metal. There are also sanding, flap sanding, and foam abrasive disks for sanding and polishing metal and other materials. You can also get carbide and diamond cup wheels for shaping metal, wood, bone, and even stone.

While there are many benefits to the angle grinder, there are some drawbacks as well. First is that most angle grinders are very loud and require ear protection. That's one major drawback that can make using an angle grinder with minimal space hard without soundproofing. The angle grinder also has a steeper learning curve when doing precise grinding and shaping because it is either held in the hand or when secured to a work surface, there are no built in tables and guides.

An angle grinder can bind and cause kickback when cutting, so be sure to have a firm grip on the tool at all times. Some grinders are pushed on and off, while others have a paddle switch that turns off when you release pressure.

Even if you do have access to other tools or end up getting more equipment, the angle grinder is still very useful. I use mine often for removing rust and scale, as well as cutting down large or odd-shaped pieces of steel. Sometimes it's easier to grind really large pieces because you bring the grinder to it, not the other way around.

Drill or Drill Press

A power hand drill or drill press is useful for drilling holes and cutting circles in steel, wood, and other materials. They can also be used to hold sanding drums, disks, and grinding stones for grinding and sanding. While a drill press does help with stability and allows for a more precise drilling of holes, a hand drill can work just as well with practice.

Make sure to use the right drill bits for the material you'll be working with. Steel and HSS (High-Speed Steel) bits work well on wood and similar materials while cobalt and carbide bits work best on steel. Cobalt and carbide bits even work on hardened steel that would ruin other bits. When drilling through metal, keep the drill as slow as practical and keep the bit cool with a cutting lubricant or beeswax.

We'll be doing quite a bit with an electric hand drill. They can be found fairly inexpensively and have many uses. Drilling, milling, grinding, sanding, and polishing can all be done with a power drill with different attachments.

Bench Grinder and Buffer

A bench grinder is basically a motor with an arbor that accepts various grind stones and other attachments. Like an angle grinder, a bench grinder can be used for almost every step in knifemaking by using different stones, sanding disks, sanding wheels, cutting disks, and wire wheels. While not as flexible as the angle grinder, the stability of a fixed bench grinder can greatly help with consistency when grinding and finishing. Bench grinders tend to be a little quieter and less messy than angle grinders.

Buffers are similar to the bench grinder but instead of grinding wheels, they are usually fitted with cloth or fiber buffing wheels. When loaded with the appropriate compound, buffing wheels can smooth, finish, and polish steel and other materials. A good buffer is important if you want to put a true mirror polish on your knives.

Bench grinders and buffers rotate very fast, so you have to be very careful when grinding or buffing as the wheel can grab whatever you are holding and throw it at high speed. This is especially true of buffing, polishing, and wire wheels. Always use the grinder and buffer with the point of the knife facing down, not up because the tip is more likely to catch on the wheel when pointing up.

Rotary Tool

Small rotary tools and rotary handpieces are great for detail work and can be used to drill holes, grind, cut, and sand various materials. A small rotary tool can even be used to cut knife blanks and used for much of the grinding, shaping and finishing. This makes it ideal for a knife maker with limited space as they are small and fairly quiet.

Belt Sander and Grinder

There are many types of belt sanders, with ones made for grinding metal called belt grinders. Sanders with wide belts are great for shaping and smoothing larger pieces of wood, but narrower belts of 1 to 2 inches are good for shaping knives and handles. While not used in this book, belt grinders can make grinding and finishing a blade very quick and efficient.

The small 1x30 inch belt sander pictured is a good entry level grinder for making knives. It's also great for sharpening blades, whether just establishing an edge or producing a mirror polished edge. Most large 2x72 inch knife grinders are fairly expensive but do a very good job at removing material. Some allow for grinding on multiple parts of the grinder to produce flat, convex, and hollow grinds.

Power Saws

There are a few different types of saws that can help speed up cutting through both soft and hard material. A scroll saw is great for cutting smaller pieces of wood and other soft material while most reciprocating saws can also cut through steel as well. Band saws are also useful for cutting curves as well as cutting straight lines and ripping boards into thinner stock for handles.

If you plan on using a band saw for cutting metal, make sure to look for a metal cutting or variable speed saw. Wood cutting band saws run pretty fast at anywhere from about 500 to 2,500 FPM (feet per minute). Metal cutting saws usually run much slower, anywhere from 90 to 450 FPM. Using a saw that runs too fast on steel can be very dangerous.

Chop, miter, table, and handheld circular saws are good for cutting material to length. Table and handheld saws can also be used to rip boards. While most of these saws are intended for cutting only wood and softer materials, they can be fitted with abrasive cutting disks for cutting steel and hard materials.

Hand Tools

Files

Whether you plan on working without power tools or have a whole shop full of equipment, a good set of files is essential for making knives. Files and rasps come in a variety of shapes for cutting and filing different shapes and profiles. They can be used to shape many different materials and sometimes only a file can get into small or curved areas.

Rasps work best on wood and soft materials and work by cutting or tearing material away. There are also different types of files ranging from coarse toothed to very fine. These can be used for smoothing rasped surfaces as well as for stock removal and shaping on metal. Small needle files also come in handy for shaping small details, fitting guards and bolsters, and cleaning up drilled holes.

Saws

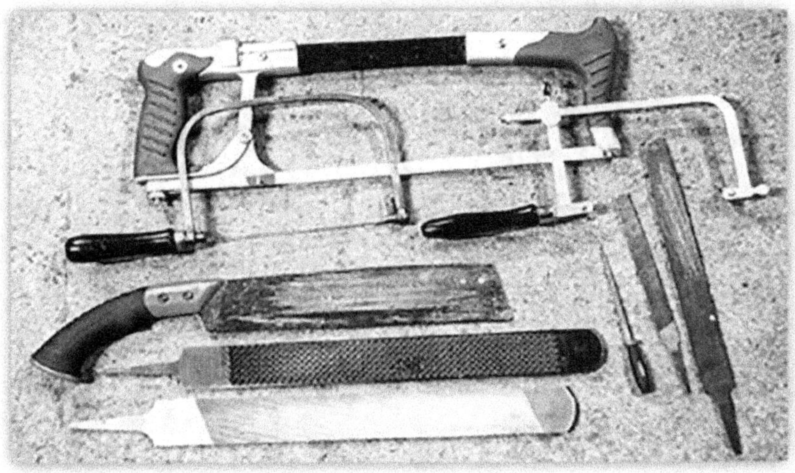

I like to have a hacksaw for cutting metal and other materials, especially for doing any trimming or initial shaping without power tools. Along with standard steel and bi-metal blades, there are also carbide coated rods that fit in a hacksaw frame. These are perfect for use as a file and for cutting hardened steel and other tough material.

Other types of saws are useful, especially when working without powered saws and grinders. Coping saws are great for doing detail cutting in softer metals and other materials. Both push and pull cut saws are great for trimming handle slabs down to size, with finer bladed saws perfect for trimming pins and exposed rivets on knife handles.

Sandpaper and Abrasives

Sandpaper is very useful for smoothing out, defining shapes, and finishing many materials. There are many types of grit used, different types of backing, different glues, and most types come in various grit sizes. Sandpaper is available in sheets, rolls and in a variety of shapes for different tasks or fitting onto sanders.

Wet/dry sandpaper can be used wet with either water or light oil and is great for smoothing and finishing steel. Using the sandpaper wet helps keep the sandpaper from clogging and lets the paper work longer before dulling.

Abrasive stones are great for grinding even hardened steel. These can be used in place of a file when working hardened steel with hand tools and can also be used to flatten and smooth out grinding marks before sanding when files won't cut it.

Fiber, steel wool, and foam abrasives are great for finishing and cleaning up surfaces. Steel wool and abrasive pads can be used to put a fine finish on softer materials as well as steel. 3M's Scotch Brite pads and wheels are very good at blending sanding marks and putting a satin finish on steel and other metals.

Vises and Clamps

Vices and clamps are very helpful when making knives, especially during otherwise dangerous operations. Securing the workpiece in a vise or with clamps especially when grinding or drilling holes keeps the piece from spinning or flying loose. They also come in handy when you need an extra hand to hold something in place.

CONCLUSION

Whilst learning a craft, in a way, the craft learns you. Spending the time to bring a beautiful object into the world might make you start to notice the world around you in a different light. You might become entranced by the simple beauty of old rusty things. You might focus in on the smallest part of an ornate gate and wonder "ah, but I wonder how they did *that* part". You might start to feel sick in supermarkets when you see how cheap and disposable industrial techniques have made the precious things you've learned to make with your own two hands.

It might make you realise how disconnected we've become from the world, the things that inhabit it. It might you wonder what's really important, to question what is necessary in this life, and who tells you that it is.

Don't let anyone ever say that learning with your hands is something people do because they're not smart enough to go to school, to become a doctor, or faceless executive at a faceless company. Craft has built the most fundamental and important aspects of our society and culture- from weaving baskets and bags to carry food and our children. To weaving our clothes and tending the land. To the creation of hand tools so fundamental, they've been with us for millennia, nearly unchanged yet ever-seeming new.

Of course, that mean making knives: something *you* now know how to do.

The most important thing to remember when creating anything is always to use extremely safe practices to avoid harming yourself and others. The tools and equipment used in all of the projects in this book can cause injury and death if they are not used correctly. Safety is a massive issue when it comes to metalwork and should not be taken lightly.

The best thing to do is to have an experienced welder or forger available, depending on the type of work you are doing, assisting you while you are learning this valuable trade. You should only attempt to work on your own once you are an experienced handler of the tools that are needed. You should always have fire safety and first aid kits available to you when working.

One important thing to note is that blacksmithing is not like many other hobbies where you can just jump straight in and start on something. Much of the equipment is very specialist and cannot be found in your local hardware store. A forge come with many safety warning and can be dangerous.

Providing that you follow the safety procedures and manufacturer's instructions on the tools you are using, metal work can be an excellent hobby and a constructive trade to know. Should something happen and you need the skills to make things yourself, knowing how to forge and how to weld can be extremely valuable trades to know.

As we mentioned in the introduction, if something did ever happen and we were no longer able to import cheap goods from around the world, knowing these skills will make you an important person. It will also improve your chances of surviving in any situation that might arise. If you are intent on making a career from it, and people still do, a farrier can be very well paying job and there are plenty of ways to make money by selling your metal creations.

You might even get good at these trades and be able to make some money from it, selling your artistic goods to shops and individuals at markets and events. You can be extremely artistic when creating with metal, and you can get good at it if you keep practicing.

Even if you don't intend to use your new skills to turn a profit, making things from metal can be a worthwhile hobby. You can make unique pieces for your home that will look artistic, rustic, or modern, depending on your mood, and they will be something that you are proud of having. When friends come over to your house, you can say, proudly, 'I made that' and they will probably say 'But it is made out of metal!' and you can then explain the world of metalwork.

www.ingramcontent.com/pod-product-compliance
Lightning Source LLC
Chambersburg PA
CBHW072234150726
48002CB00005B/2078